8½ SECRETS

HOW TO KEEP, ENCOURAGE AND **STOP** DRIVING YOUR VOLUNTEERS CRAZY

June Kenny
"Empowering Christian Leadership"

Scripture quotations marked NIV are taken from THE HOLY BIBLE, NEW INTERNATIONAL VERSION®. Copyright © 1973, 1978, 1984 International Bible Society. Used by permission of Zondervan. All rights reserved.

Scripture quotations marked NLT are taken from The Holy Bible, New Living Translation, copyright 1996. Used by permission of Tyndale House Publishers, Inc., Wheaton, Illinois 60189. All rights reserved.

Scripture quotations marked ESV are taken from The ESV® Bible (The Holy Bible, English Standard Version®). Copyright © 2001 by Crossway Bibles, a publishing ministry of Good News Publishers. All rights reserved.

Copyright © 2016 by June Kenny

All rights reserved. With the exception of any of the training support materials, no part of this publication may be reproduced, stored in a retrieval system, or transmitted in any form or by any means – electronic, mechanical, photocopy, recording, or any other – except for brief quotations in printed or digital reviews without the prior written permission of the author.

ISBN-13: 978-1536962178
ISBN-10: 1536962171

LifeCare Publishing is a branch of
LifeCare Christian Center
A non-profit faith-based ministry
www.LifeCareChristianCenter.org
info.lifecarecc@gmail.com
Westland, MI USA

Mission Statement
LifeCare Christian Center exists to partner with individuals, churches and the community in promoting spiritual, emotional, physical and relational wholeness by providing quality, affordable care, education and training services from a Christian perspective.

For bulk quantity discounted purchases, contact us at
Info.LifecareCC@gmail.com or 734-629-3551.

ENDORSEMENTS

JOHN OELZE
Executive Pastor, First MB Church, Wichita, KS
www.firstmbchurch.org

> *"Having served alongside June Kenny in ministry with the responsibility of overseeing 500+ volunteers in my ministry area alone, I often sought out June's insights with volunteer development. More than just another book to be read and then placed on the shelf, **8½ SECRETS** is packed with worksheets and practical handouts that you'll come back to again and again to equip others to increase their leadership skills. If you are just starting off in ministry, **this book is a must read** in helping you understand how to work with volunteers. For the seasoned leader, this tool will sharpen your leadership and volunteer edge. The section on **The Top Ten Reasons Why Volunteers Quit** was worth it alone."*

LILLIAN EASTERLY-SMITH
Founder/Director of LifeCare Christian Center
www.lifecarechristiancenter.org

> *"**8½ SECRETS** should be read and referred back to as an invaluable resource for EVERY Ministry Leader! I highly recommend it. June Kenny has captured all the key ingredients for a sustainable volunteer base as well as how to do it with practical steps, detail and encouragement to the reader. Not only have I enjoyed reading through the information here but have personally used the techniques and strategies she has presented to our teams in various workshops over the years. June Kenny, with all her insight, personal and professional experience and expertise, has made a huge impact in our ministry."*

WENDELL BROWNING
Men's Ministry Leader, Oak Pointe Church, Novi, MI
www.oakpointe.org

> *"**8½ SECRETS** is a very detailed and life-changing book that, if implemented, will truly benefit paid staff and volunteer leaders. I highly recommend it to church leaders. Your volunteers will be impacted for life!"*

Participant Comments from
Christian Leadership Training Programs:

- *"We need to see more of this type of training. This not only helps us to be more effective with our volunteers but also in our family & professional lives!"* J.U., Volunteer Leader, Recovery Ministry (church, 12,000 attendees)

- *"June Kenny was first rate, knowledgeable and spoke with precision and confidence. June was both inspiring and motivational."* G.E.H., Pastor and D.Min. Candidate, Ashland Seminary

- *"This workshop makes me see my co-workers differently–gives me strategies to work better with them. Thanks!"* E.M.W., Church Administrative Team (church 500 attendees)

- *"June Kenny was dynamic, motivating and thought-provoking!"* G.P.C., Board Member, Christian Non-Profit

- *"We're blessed to have June Kenny. This was a tremendous program–very understandable and the presentation was outstanding."* W.B., Volunteer Leader, Recovery Ministry (church of 2,000)

- *"The concepts were simple...but profound. Not so difficult in steps...that I can't 'remember' to do them in the future...and with practice hopefully will be easier."* J.B., Pastoral staff member (church of 3,000+)

- *"Each topic had its own distinctive leadership enhancement element. It was clear that the materials had been well researched and had a high degree of validity and reliability."* Executive Team member, Salvation Army Adult Rehabilitation Center (A.R.C.), Detroit

8½ SECRETS

CONTENTS

TOP SECRET:	*How to Get the Most Value from this Book*	7
SECRET #1:	*Maximize the Power of Your Volunteer Resource*	11
SECRET #2:	*Encourage with Credibility When Things Go Right*	35
SECRET #3:	*Give Compassionate Criticism When Things Go Wrong—You Owe it to Your Volunteers to Tell Them*	53
SECRET #4:	*Make Your Expectations Clear to Get the Results You Want*	79
SECRET #5:	*Run Meetings that Don't Drive Your Volunteers Crazy (or Away!)*	97
SECRET #6:	*Tap into Built-In Enthusiasm*	119
SECRET #7:	*Restructure Volunteer Opportunities to Expand Your Volunteer Base*	147
SECRET #8:	*Lead with Humility— Listen More, Talk Less*	177
SECRET #8½:	*Strategically PLAN to Succeed!*	207
SECRET #9:	**BONUS!**	**229**

How to Get the Most Value from this Book

Congratulations! You have just picked up a book that can make a qualitative difference in your ministry if you have and use Volunteers (which should roughly be about 100% of you).

8½ SECRETS will benefit all who are on the front lines of ministry—even if you are a Volunteer yourself. Paid or unpaid, if you lead Volunteers, this book will help you sharpen your leadership skills and offer creative ideas for meeting the challenges of ministry management. **Why do I call these ideas SECRETS?** It is because I seldom see them consistently practiced in churches, Christian organizations, or anywhere for that matter. I have also personally talked with hundreds of Volunteers who happen to agree. I am confident that Ministry Leaders are dedicated, hard-working and want to positively impact the world for Christ. Therefore, I can only conclude THESE IDEAS MUST BE A SECRET! Surely, if not, more Christian leaders would already be doing this, right?

This book does more than divulge the secrets; it includes the important how-to strategies to successfully implement each one. In fact, *8½ SECRETS* can be used as a refresher for experienced Ministry Leaders, training for Volunteer Leaders or a self-study for anyone that you are encouraging to step into leadership.

8½ SECRETS is dedicated to giving you and your Volunteer management team the basic tools it needs to get everyone *off the bench* and *into the game*. This book may not be everything in the world that leaders need to know, but they **NEED TO KNOW EVERYTHING IN THIS BOOK.**

Some important topics include:

- **How to keep the great volunteers you already have**
- **How to run meetings that don't drive your Volunteers crazy**
- **How to tap into built-in enthusiasm**
- **How to give compassionate criticism when things go wrong**
- **How to restructure your Volunteer opportunities to expand participation**
- **How to assess and strengthen your leadership skills**
- **And much more**

You will learn how to create a Volunteer-friendly environment that attracts those who have not yet found a reason to *get off of the bench*. Imagine what could be accomplished for God's Kingdom if we called for 100% participation and they actually came. What a concept! Challenging? Scary? Yes, but a great problem to have.

Does it feel like you are engaged in a never-ending recruitment process? Do Volunteers drop out more quickly than expected? The cure will surprise you. To get more Volunteers, laser focus on the ones you already have. Why? Those Volunteers will be more effective. They will stay longer, doing the right things, and you will not be spinning in that same old revolving door. And those committed Volunteers will become your most effective recruitment tool to expand your Volunteer base.

TOP SECRET: *How to Get the Most Value from this Book*

---

*To get more Volunteers, laser focus on
the ones you already have.*

What specifically could you be doing in the here and now to take care of the Volunteers you already have? You are in luck. The secrets you find in this book are effective, practical and powerful. Fortunately for all of us, taking care of Volunteers is attainable.

Many of the great ideas for successful Volunteer leadership come directly from Scripture, others are consistent with Biblical principles. 8½ SECRETS includes simple, profound how-to strategies in down-to-earth language making them easy to understand and implement.

8½ SECRETS is meant to be written in, highlighted, earmarked and kept as a handy reference for when you need to handle those inevitable challenging moments. Read this book in any order that makes sense to you. Pick and choose the bits and pieces that apply to your unique situation.

You can use the book in whatever way helps you best:

- **an idea generator**
- **a discussion starter**
- **a personal notebook**
- **team development**
- **a training manual for staff and team leaders**
- **a welcome gift for new or *wanna-be* Volunteer leaders**

Please allow me the privilege of encouraging you to start with ***SECRET #2: Encouragement*** and ***SECRET #3: Compassionate Criticism***. Tackle these first and you will have mastered two of the most fundamental leadership skills you can acquire.

You have permission to duplicate any of the training support materials you need to help you stay on track as you engage in on-going recruitment and Volunteer development. There will always be an endless supply of new Volunteers and Volunteer leaders that need the basics.

I have been working with churches since 1998, and corporations and non-profits for over twenty-five years. What have I discovered? Volunteers are an under-used and under-appreciated resource while paid staff typically find themselves exhausted, stressed-out and on the way to burning out. It takes a well-designed and well-executed plan to maximize the potential of any workforce. How many churches and Christian non-profits have that? Not many. Most are *winging it*, operating in crisis mode, or playing catch-up with needs. If that sounds like your organization, please know it does not have to be that way. This book will help you create your unique strategy for making the most of your most valuable resource—your Volunteers.

Good luck and enjoy the journey!

#1: Maximize the Power of Your Volunteer Resource

So, how do we do that?

> **ESCAPE CLAUSE:** If you have enough high-quality Volunteers and the financial support for their *care and feeding*, you can TEMPORARILY **STOP RIGHT HERE**. Please go directly to **SECRET #2: Encouragement** or **SECRET #3: Compassionate Criticism** – the **two most important skills** every ministry leader needs to have down pat. You can always come back later to see if you are utilizing your Volunteer resources to the max.

Does it seem like you are forever recruiting to fill the same Volunteer positions? Maybe a shortage of Volunteers is not your issue.

Do you wonder if you are using your Volunteers in ways that make the most of their talents, skills and spiritual gifts?

Do you find yourself frustrated trying to schedule and keep track of all of your Volunteers?

Do you sometimes find there are too many Volunteers with too little for each to do?

If any of these questions have entered your mind, you are not alone. Volunteers can sometimes feel like a mixed blessing. They ease our workload but make more work for us on the management side. They work for free but they cost money to support, appreciate and train.

Ask yourself these key questions: Do we really need Volunteers in the first place? Are they worth it? How do we know if the benefit outweighs the cost? This chapter will help you find those answers.

Why do you need Volunteers? There are at least eight distinct benefits Volunteers could bring to your ministry. How many immediately pop into your mind? To prime the pump, the first two are filled in for you.

EIGHT DISTINCT BENEFITS OF HAVING VOLUNTEERS:

1. **Volunteers Increase Results** (more hands on deck = more work done)

2. **Volunteers Expand Virtual Budget** (hours of labor = money, if you had to pay)

WHAT ELSE CAN VOLUNTEERS DO FOR YOU?

3. _____

4. _____

5. _____

6. _____

7. _____

8. _____

Let us take a closer look at each one of these. Maybe one or more will resonate with your unique situation and make you happy that God has blessed you with Volunteers.

Benefits #1 & #2: VOLUNTEERS INCREASE RESULTS AND EXPAND YOUR VIRTUAL BUDGET

Could we be doing as much without our Volunteer workforce? After all, more hands equal more output. But do we know how

SECRET #1: *Maximize the Power of Your Volunteer Resource*

much more work we are talking about? It is possible to get a clearer picture. For example, how many hours per week, month or year are actually being contributed to your ministry? You might be surprised by the results. I know I was.

When I was working as Director of Volunteer and Staff Development at a large church of 14,000, we conservatively estimated that our 2,000 Volunteers contributed 260,000 work-hours per year. That number was not pulled out of thin air. It was a conservative estimate based on a 2.5 hours per week per Volunteer. Of course there were Volunteers who contributed less, but we had a huge component that contributed between 10 and 20 hours per week. Many others worked on projects that demanded massive short-term time commitments—mission trips at home and abroad, summer children's programs, retreats, counselors at summer camps, and Christmas and Easter programs, to name a few. What do you think is a realistic guess-timate for your ministry or organization?

Here is a simple method to calculate the hourly contribution and monetary impact to your ministry budget. Be realistic and be sure to include the prep time necessary to do an excellent job. Your pastor delivers a 20-45 minute talk each Sunday (depending on your denomination). Did you think the message pops into his head as he walks to the microphone? Hardly. Volunteers seldom *wing it* any more than paid staff. They want to do a good job. For example, Sunday School teachers have pre-class tasks to complete. Even baking a cake for a church luncheon requires shopping, cooking, and delivering time. Preparing the craft materials for twenty 4-year-olds does not happen by magic either.

First, figure out how many work-hours of Volunteer service you are currently receiving to achieve each ministry task. The key to getting our arms around this amorphous thing called Volunteer Contribution is to focus on the tasks rather than the people. This calculation will probably take the longest but will be worth the effort. The data you uncover will not only surprise you but help you persuade the decision makers that there is wisdom in budgeting more funds for Volunteer *care and feeding*.

Identify each on-going, predictable ministry task. Every church has dozens (hundreds?) of on-going tasks. Some tasks involve only thirty minutes per week per person, others much more. Some involve only one or two Volunteers, others dozens. For example, if you have six people greeting visitors per service and each one has a thirty-minute shift, you have been blessed with three hours of Volunteer labor per service. If you have two services, it jumps to six hours. Six hours per week amounts 312 hours annually. Once you know how many work-hours are needed to successfully accomplish each on-going ministry task, you can tally them to guess-timate the annual Volunteer workload of your ministry as a whole.

At some point you are going to want to keep track of how many Volunteers are involved. In the greeter example above, twelve different Volunteers work each Sunday but they may be assigned only two Sundays a month. In that case, you are looking at a total of 24 Volunteers to accomplish this single task each month. The labor-hours remain fixed whether 6 or 48 individuals are involved. For our purposes right now, however, we do not need Volunteer quantity. We are trying to measure impact to your ministry and expansion of your virtual budget.

Second, calculate work-hours needed for special projects, short-term ministry events, etc. (i.e., anything that has a beginning, a middle and an end). Some of these events or projects may occur only once per year (i.e., Christmas and Easter programs, Summer Bible Camps, Fall Kick-Off, Volunteer Appreciation Week, etc.) Others may occur seasonally (i.e., Spring and Fall clean up, flower planting, Summer Picnics).

Third, if you have not already included your Volunteer board members, deacons and other administrative-type Volunteers,

SECRET #1: *Maximize the Power of Your Volunteer Resource*

calculate the number of hours they provide. It is all too easy to forget the Volunteers who work behind the scenes on the planning side rather than the front-line delivery side of ministry.

Use the information in **APPENDICES 1A and 1B Worksheets** at the end of the chapter to help you calculate the labor-hours that your ministry uses annually. Surprise yourself. Be thrilled by how much your Volunteers have actually been doing. Imagine if you had to do it all without them. If you would like to check out how one Volunteer leader at a large Atlanta church calculated the Volunteer hours of her M.O.P.S. ministry (Mothers of Pre-Schoolers), see **APPENDIX 1C**.

Actual Impact to Budget: What was the estimated monetary value at the church of 14,000 I referenced earlier? We used a very modest $10/hr rate[1] calculating that our Volunteers contributed over two and a half million dollars per year. No church benefactor writes that large of a check each year. Many of our Volunteers used skills that should have been valued at a much higher hourly rate. For example: plumbers, carpenters, accountants, musicians, artists, project managers, teachers, lawyers, seamstresses, IT technicians, video experts, marriage counselors, grief counselors, etc. Free does not mean without value, and when it comes to your Volunteers, free does not exactly mean free either. There is a cost to resourcing this unpaid workforce if you want to maximize their impact.

Once you have tallied the total labor hours of your ministry, calculate the estimated impact to your budget. Perhaps under-estimated would be a more accurate term. If we actually had to pay fair labor prices for the expertise we have received, minimum wage would not even come close. Even so, just for grins, calculate your total anyway. Your budget might look more impressive than you first thought.

Simply counting Volunteers and getting an accurate number

---

[1] A 2009 *Stanford Social Innovation Review* reported that volunteer labor was valued at almost $20.00/hour.

can present a problem for some organizations. At one church I worked with, we asked each Ministry Leader to compile a list of current Volunteers so we could identify who they were and how many we had. It is embarrassing to say, but we had some dearly departed still on our list. And, sadder yet, some of the current Volunteers who had been working for over a year were not on the list at all. Hopefully, that is not the picture at your church.

So, who are your Volunteers? Do you have an accurate and up-to-date list? Take a moment right now and make one. (Helpful hint: Please include only those who have not yet been *called up yonder*.) Or make the commitment to meet with your ministry team and compile such a list ASAP. **APPENDIX 1D** will help you get started if you do not have tracking software in place. Many churches and Christian non-profits diligently track Volunteer service as well as work hours so that their appreciation efforts more accurately reflect the service rendered. A "Thank You" always rings with more truth when Volunteers know that you actually know what they did.

How can we support and appreciate our Volunteers if we do not have an accurate idea of who is doing what, how often and for how long? The answer is we can't. When Volunteers become invisible to us, we run the risk that they will not be our Volunteers for long. It is one of the big reasons Volunteers leave. And, unfortunately, they not only walk; they talk. It becomes much more difficult to recruit new Volunteers when you have developed a negative reputation for how you treat the current Volunteers God has brought you.

EIGHT DISTINCT VOLUNTEER BENEFITS

1. Volunteers Increase Results
2. Volunteers Expand Virtual Budget

3. **Volunteers Provide Ministry Diversity**
4. **Volunteers Give More Money than Non-Volunteers**
5. **Volunteers Make Recruiting New Volunteers Easier**
6. **Volunteers Expand Your Social Capital**
7. **Volunteers Become Your Goodwill Ambassadors**
8. **Volunteers Help You Fulfill Your Real Ministry Purpose**

Benefit #3: VOLUNTEERS PROVIDE MINISTRY DIVERSITY

God gives each of us talents to help others and to further His Kingdom goals. I also believe He gives us un-talents—skills that we earnestly desire but will never possess. Others must provide them for us. It forces us to realize how much we need each other—all the body parts are essential and important.[2] For example, music is very important to me. It is my primary spiritual pathway. However, (God's sense of humor?) I cannot carry a tune in a bucket. Even though it is my job to be a professional communicator, I know that I will never be able to connect with people using one of the most powerful tools—music. I definitely need all of those wonderful, musically gifted people. By the way, most of them are Volunteers.

How wide and diverse could your ministry be if you had the benefit of all the talent *sitting on the bench*? At one church, an Autistic Children's Ministry provided Volunteers to work with autistic children, one-on-one, so that parents could attend the worship service and receive some much-needed spiritual nourishment. What talents, skills, spiritual gifts and passions are still *sitting on the benches* where you are? Volunteers can do all of the things we do not have the time, energy, talent, heart or finances to do—if we would only ask them.

---

[2] I Corinthians 12:12

8½ SECRETS

Benefit #4: VOLUNTEERS GIVE MORE MONEY THAN NON-VOLUNTEERS

Volunteers contribute financially at a higher rate than non-Volunteers. They just do. A recent research study conducted by Fidelity Charitable Gift Fund found that Volunteers contributed an average of ten times more money than non-Volunteers.[3] They commit not only their time and talent but their treasure as well. "For where your treasure is, there your heart will be also."[4] The reverse seems also to be true. "Where your heart is...."

In one large church in Atlanta, the M.O.P.S. (Mothers of Pre-Schoolers) Coordinator was trying to find a way to make it possible for every young mother to attend every meeting. As an evangelistic outreach program, M.O.P.S. attracted women from the community as well as church members. In the past, each participating mother was required to skip at least one meeting per semester to work in childcare in order to make the program economically feasible. This Coordinator creatively thought to ask the mentor moms if they might be willing to pay their own required National registration fees to provide the extra money for childcare. She also sought the aid of real, live grandmothers to be *Rocker Moms* for the infant rooms reducing the number of paid workers. The new plan succeeded. Mentor moms willingly offered to pay for themselves when they learned that their money would make it possible for all of the young moms to attend every session. *Rocker Moms*, a.k.a. grandma*s*, were excited about the opportunity to hug babies two mornings a month, especially when they knew they were also providing a genuine blessing to the younger moms. A win-win solution!

---

[3] Fidelity® Charitable Gift Fund, et. al., "Fidelity® Charitable Gift Fund and VolunteerMatch Form Alliance and Release Landmark Study on Volunteering," *BusinessWire.com*, 03 Dec. 2009.
[4] Matthew 6:21/Luke 12:34, NIV

SECRET #1: *Maximize the Power of Your Volunteer Resource*

Benefit #5: VOLUNTEERS MAKE RECRUITING NEW VOLUNTEERS EASIER

Volunteers will recruit new Volunteers. That is, they do if they love what they are doing and feel the blessing that comes from being engaged in God's work. Your leadership is the critical factor here. Do you help them connect with the importance of what God is doing through their ministry? Do you love, support and care about them as people rather than merely replaceable worker-bees?

Volunteers talk with friends and family about what excites and energizes them. Excitement is contagious and attracts others to join in. People intrinsically want to be part of something bigger than themselves and something that is making a positive difference. What is bigger than God? And who makes a bigger positive impact in the world? It helps, too, if you intentionally encourage them to share their passion, excitement and positive impact stories with others.

Benefit #6: VOLUNTEERS EXPAND YOUR SOCIAL CAPITAL

Churches have their share of worldly issues to deal with: zoning ordinances, parking expansion resistance and a need for unique ministry resources. An expansive and committed human network can facilitate success in surprising ways.

A mid-sized church of 400 was struggling to break through the barrier from one to two services. They had tried to implement the change multiple times and failed. Fortunately, the father of one active member happened to be a professional market analyst. When he heard of their difficulty, he offered his services free-of-charge in order to help the church administration better understand the obstacles and create the needed strategies to successfully expand their reach into the community.

Influencing a zoning board, donating gifts for a teen auction to pay for camp scholarships, photographing members for a church directory, and providing sports equipment for afterschool recreation, just to name a few, have all been made possible through networking with people who attend, volunteer and care about their church. Anything you need to support your ministry goals is out there for the asking. Your Volunteers are the key. Where you cannot ask, they can. Where you cannot open doors, they can. The more Volunteers you have, the more keys you have at your disposal to unlock the support and resources you need.

Benefit #7: VOLUNTEERS BECOME YOUR GOODWILL AMBASSADORS

Volunteers take the stories of your good works to friends and neighbors and draw them to your organization—physically, spiritually and financially. It helps, of course, if they are encouraged and trained to know how to do this. This kind of *storytelling* is not only a learnable skill, it is a very effective marketing and fundraising tool that even the most bashful Volunteer can embrace because they will be talking about something they love.

Benefit #8: VOLUNTEERS HELP YOU FULFILL YOUR REAL MINISTRY PURPOSE

Matthew 28:19-20 tells us to "go and make disciples." How do I know this is your real purpose? Because it is the purpose/commandment for all of us. As a Ministry Leader, however, you happen to be in the ideal spot to fulfill it right here, right now. Serving in the center of God's plan is one of the fast-tracks of spiritual development. What are you currently doing to encourage your Volunteers to deepen their love and understanding of God? Have you been able to incorporate support of their spiritual journey as they go about the ministry tasks designed to support others? Or do you see them as simply replaceable worker-bees?

SECRET #1: *Maximize the Power of Your Volunteer Resource*

I Corinthians 12:7 states, "Now to each one the manifestation of the Spirit is given for the common good." Verse 27 continues, "Now you are the body of Christ, and each one of you is a part of it." And my personal favorite, Ephesians 2:10, "For we are God's handiwork, created in Christ Jesus to do good works, which God prepared in advance for us to do." Since it seems clear that all of us are called to participate, not merely *spectate*, the more important

> *"Do I have a responsibility to create more opportunities that invite the non-participant into God's work... for the sake of their spiritual development?"*

question for leaders to embrace is "Do I have a responsibility to create more opportunities that invite the non-participant into God's work—not just for the sake of the work I need to do but for the sake of their spiritual development?"

Using *Pareto's 80/20 Principle* as a guideline, your organization is about average if you have 20% of your congregation serving and 80% sitting in the pews as spectators. Do you know what your current engagement rate is? Would ministry benefit if it were higher? Our ultimate purpose might better be achieved by partnering with Volunteers for their sakes as well as what they can do. And what they can do will amaze you!

Do any of the eight reasons resonate with your situation or reinforce your thinking? I hope you have renewed your appreciation of your Volunteers, what they contribute to your ministry and what this ministry does for their hearts and souls. It is a match made in heaven.

Ask yourself: "What do I really think about my Volunteers? Do I really need and value them? Do I actually know the extent of their impact?" What is truly important to us rarely stays hidden for long.

Volunteers will quickly figure out if we value them or not.

When any organization really wants its values known, it removes the guesswork. The Walt Disney organization shows that it unquestionably values its customers by calling them *Guests*. Using the term Guest is not a superficial gesture. We typically take better care of *Guests*. Even capitalizing the word makes an important difference in the minds of the *Cast Members* (i.e., employees). Would you look at your Volunteers differently if they were your Partners in Ministry? Might Partners more likely be:

- included in decision making?
- given significant or challenging tasks to accomplish?
- formally praised and recognized?
- resourced to be successful?
- held accountable?
- trained to grow their skills and value to the ministry?

If your Volunteers are already an integral part of your ministry's success, or you want them to be from now on, the rest of this book is my gift to you. It will show you how to take better care of the ones you have now and ways to intentionally expand this God-given resource. I hope you will consider sharing some of the creative things you are doing and how you are taking care of your Volunteers. We can learn from you. Be sure to take a look at **SECRET #8½: Strategically PLAN to Succeed!** to see how you can be a blessing to others. God promised Abram, "...I will bless you...and you will be a blessing...and all peoples on earth will be blessed through you."[5] We have the same promise and opportunity today.

> *"Alone we can do so little; together we can do so much."*
> *− Helen Keller*

---

[5] Genesis 12:2-3, NIV

SECRET #1: *Maximize the Power of Your Volunteer Resource*

☑ Action Steps to Maximize Value:

☐ **1.** Calculate the total annual Volunteer labor-hours that are needed by your ministry. Start by identifying the individual tasks. Then calculate how many work-hours are needed to successfully complete each task. Ideally, tabulating the total for all ministry areas in your entire organization is a great idea, too. It will give you powerful ammunition for gaining organization-wide support for a more effective Volunteer Support System. See **Appendices 1A and 1B Worksheets** to get started. See **Appendix 1C** to see how one ministry approached this challenge.

☐ **2.** Calculate the monetary impact to your virtual budget. (This will make you feel good.) See **Appendix 1A,** Question #8.

☐ **3.** Hug the next Volunteer you see and tell them how much you appreciate partnering with them in God's work! (See *SECRET #2* for more ideas.) Start by listing who they are: Use **Appendix 1D** to get started.

☐ **4.** Go to www.JuneKenny.com for free training Worksheets and helpful tips on working with Volunteers.

"True faith manifests itself through actions."
– Francis Chan

☑ Actions I Plan to Take to Maximize Value:

1. _____

2. _____

3. _____

4. _____

5. _____

6. _____

7. _____

8. _____

"Volunteers aren't paid; not because they are worthless, but because they are PRICELESS!"
— *Sherry Ruth Anderson*

APPENDIX 1A: *Calculate the Value of Volunteer Labor*

How to Calculate the Value of Volunteer Labor

10 Important Questions to Consider

1. What is the specific event, task, project, or ministry job I want to tally?

    For example:

Weekly women's ministry Bible study, worship service greeters, typing and printing weekly bulletins, vacation Bible school day camp, children's Christmas concert, Maundy Thursday brunch, etc.

2. How many different roles/jobs are identifiable? List them.

    For example:

Childcare, greeters, hospitality, performers, speakers, table leaders, set up, clean up, etc.

3. What is the unit of time I want to measure?

    For example:

One meeting or one event, one month, one worship service, etc.

4. How many people are needed to perform each job/role during that time period?

    For example:

Childcare (8), greeters (6), speakers (3), table leaders (8), set up (6), clean-up (6)

APPENDIX 1A: *Calculate the Value of Volunteer Labor*

5. Look at each job separately. How many hours does the Volunteer work per time unit?

For example:

A childcare worker* is present during the 2-hr meeting plus 15 minutes before and after. Total = 2.5 hours per meeting per childcare worker. One meeting requires 8 childcare workers X 2.5 hours each equaling 20 labor hours per meeting.

*FYI: <u>Count all childcare workers</u> even if you are paying them. These workers are contributing labor hours necessary for the success of your event. And who knows? Someday they might all be Volunteers.

6. Are paid church staff involved in the event/project? Should I include their labor?

Answer:

If the staff person is only functioning in their specific staff role, **the answer is NO**. If they have stepped in to perform hands-on labor that other Volunteers are also doing (or could do), **the answer is YES**. They are filling in because not enough Volunteers were in place. The goal of tallying is to understand the labor requirements of your ministry project—regardless of who is providing the labor.

7. What should I do once I have tallied the hours for each of the <u>individual jobs</u> in my event? (hours X # of people performing a specific job)

Answer:

Once you know how many hours each job/role contributed to make your event happen, add the totals of all of the jobs to get the total for the entire event. How many of these events occur per

APPENDIX 1A: *Calculate the Value of Volunteer Labor*

year? Multiply your total by that number (of occurrences) to get the annual labor total.

Example: (see **Appendix 1C:** *Ministry Case Study*)

8. How will this information help me as a Ministry Leader?
Answer:

First. It will probably amaze and impress you that so many hands contributed to your ministry's success. It is a little humbling, too, to recognize that God is using you in mighty ways through your leadership. Genuine Volunteer appreciation will ooze through every pore!

Second. Sharing this information with pastor and staff will help shift the Volunteer Paradigm from replaceable worker to significant partner in ministry.

Third. You can also connect the dots between Volunteer/ministry partners and virtual budget. If you were to attach an arbitrary $20.00 charge per hour (or whatever the current estimate might be) and multiply by the number of labor hours used, you would definitely see an impact to your virtual budget!*

Fourth. Sharing the collective data (total hours and/or monetary impact) with the Volunteers as a group goes a long way in filling their love buckets! Most people volunteer because they want to belong to something bigger than themselves and to make a positive difference. You have just shown them in a concrete way how much they mean to your ministry! **WARNING: Please do not share individual totals** with an individual Volunteer! You have probably underestimated how much time they gave and run the risk of offending them. Stick with the grand total and public announcement for maximum impact.

*FYI: A 2009 *Stanford Social Innovation Review* reported that volunteer labor was valued at almost $20.00/hour.

27

APPENDIX 1A: *Calculate the Value of Volunteer Labor*

9. How often does this kind of tallying need to be done?
Answer:

If carefully done, every five years or so should be sufficient to make sure you still have a clear picture of Volunteer impact. Helpful Hint: Create a special ministry team (Volunteer led and managed, of course) for the "care and feeding of Volunteers." This might be one of their many important responsibilities. In fact, it was a Volunteer that undertook this task (**Appendix 1C:** *Ministry Case Study*) and shared it with her staff Ministry Leader.

10. How can I adjust to changing Volunteer numbers and larger events without having to start all over again?
Answer:

Once you have calculated the labor required for your overall ministry (i.e. multiple tasks, events, projects, etc.) and have identified the actual people who provided the labor, you can calculate an average per Volunteer. At one church we calculated that the church-wide average was 2 hours per week per Volunteer (or about 100 hours each per year). As the Volunteer numbers increased, we had a good estimate of the added labor hours. We guesstimated that each new Volunteer = 100 hours/year. Total estimated Volunteer hours and impact to budget* were usually shared during Volunteer Appreciation events.

APPENDIX 1B: *Calculate Ministry Labor Hours* WORKSHEET

CALCULATE MINISTRY LABOR HOURS

Ministry Area: _____ Prepared by: _____

#	TASK ↓	ROLE:	ROLE:	ROLE:
GRAND TOTAL = _____ HRS.		Total Hrs. =	Total Hrs. =	Total Hrs. =

APPENDIX 1C: *Atlanta MOPS Case Study*

Atlanta Mothers of Preschoolers (MOPS) Program
Attendance 115 Women and 85 Children X 16 Meetings, Mom's Night-Out Events
(Service Projects not included)

Appendix 1C: Case Study page 1

Tasks:	MOPS Coordinator	Asst. Coordinator	Steering Ctte. (36)	Speaker Coordinator (2)
Steering Retreat			3hr X 36 = 108	
Pre/Post-mtg. work	5 hrs			
Pre/Post-mtg. attendance	2 hrs	1 hr		
Kick Off/Registration Event			2.5hr X 36 = 90 hrs	
Pre/Post-mtg. work	1 hr			
Pre/Post Mtg. attendance	2 hrs			
Steering Reg. Mtg. X 4			2hr X 4 X 36 = 288	
Pre/Post-mtg. work	2 hrs X 2 = 4 hrs			
Pre/Post Mtg. attendance	2 hrs X 2 = 4 hrs			
Steering Post Mtg/Lunch			2hr X 36 = 72 hrs	
Pre/Post Mtg. work				
Pre/Post-mtg. attendance				
Reg.MOPS meetings X16			2hr X 36 X 16 = 1152	
Pre/Post-mtg. work	2 hrs X 16 = 36 hrs	1.5 X 9 mo. = 13.5 hrs		1 hr X 16 = 16
Pre/Post Mtg. attendance	.5 hr X 16 = 8 hrs			
Email/ Phone Contact	2 hrs per mo. X 9 = 18			
Articles for Newsletter	3 hrs X 9 = 27 hrs			
Mom's Night Out Events				
GRAND TOTAL =				
3,380.5 hrs	Total = 105 hrs	Total = 14.5 hrs	Total = 1710 hrs	Total = 16 hrs

APPENDIX 1C: *Atlanta MOPS Case Study*

Atlanta Mothers of Preschoolers (MOPS) Program
Attendance 115 Women and 85 Children X 16 Meetings, Mom's Night-Out Events
(Service Projects not included)

Tasks:	Speakers	Fund Raising (3)	Finance			
Steering Retreat						
Pre/Post-mtg. work			30 hrs pre/post			
Pre/Post-mtg. attend						
Kick Off/Registration						
Pre/Post-mtg. work						
Pre/Post Mtg. attend						
Steering Reg. Mtg. X 4						
Pre/Post-mtg. work						
Pre/Post Mtg. attend						
Steering Post Mtg/Lunch						
Pre/Post Mtg. work						
Pre/Post-mtg. attend						
Reg. MOPS meetings X16	2 hr X 16 = 36					
Pre/Post-mtg. work	3 hr X 16 = 48	3 hrs X 9 mo = 27 hrs	3 hrs X 9 mo = 27 hrs	1 hr X 16 = 16 hrs		2 hr X 9 mo X 2 = 36
Pre/Post Mtg. attend				1 hr X 4 X 16 = 64		
Email/ Phone Contact						
Articles for Newsletter						
Mom's Night Out Events						
GRAND TOTAL						
3,380.5 hrs	T = 84 hrs	Total = 27 hrs	Total = 57 hrs	Total = 80 hrs		Total = 36 hrs

31

APPENDIX 1C: *Atlanta MOPS Case Study*

Atlanta Mothers of Preschoolers (MOPS) Program
Attendance 115 Women and 85 Children X 16 Meetings, Mom's Night Out Events
(Service Projects not included)

Appendix 1C: Case Study page 3

Tasks:	Publicity	Table Leaders (13)	Crafts	Moppets Liaison	Mentor Moms (6)	Childcare (17)
Steering Retreat						
Pre/Post-mtg. work						
Pre/Post-mtg. attend						
Kick Off/Registration						
Pre/Post-mtg. work						
Pre/Post Mtg. attend						
Steering Reg. Mtg. X 4						
Pre/Post-mtg. work						
Pre/Post Mtg. attend						
Steering Post Mtg/lunch					2 hr X 4 = 8 hrs	
Pre/Post Mtg. work					1 hr X 6 = 6 hrs	
Pre/Post-mtg. attend					1 hr X 6 = 6 hrs	
Reg. MOPS meetings X 16					2hr X 16 X 4 = 128	2hr X 16 X 17 = 544
Pre/Post-mtg. work	5 hr X 9 mo = 45		2 X 9 mos = 18	1 hr X 9 mo = 9		
Pre/Post Mtg. attend						5hr X 16 X 17 = 136
Email/ Phone Contact						
Articles for Newsletter						
Mom's Night Out Events		3hr X 9 mo X 13 = 351				
GRAND TOTAL = 3,380.5 hrs	Total = 45 hrs	Total = 351 hrs	T = 18 hrs	Total = 9 hrs	T = 148 hrs	T = 680 hours

APPENDIX 1D: *Volunteer Contact Information* p. 1 of 2

VOLUNTEER CONTACT INFORMATION

Appendix 1D – page 1 of 2

	LAST NAME	FIRST NAME	CELL PHONE	TEXT Y/N	HOME PHONE	BIRTHDAY M/D/YR	EMAIL
1							
2							
3							
4							
5							
6							
7							
8							
9							
10							

APPENDIX 1D: *Volunteer Contact Information* p. 2 of 2

VOLUNTEER CONTACT INFORMATION

	LAST NAME	FIRST INITIAL	STREET	CITY	ZIP	ROLE #1	ROLE #2	ROLE #3
1								
2								
3								
4								
5								
6								
7								
8								
9								
10								

#2: Encourage with Credibility When Things Go Right

So, how do we do that?

> "Do not let any unwholesome talk
> come out of your mouths, but only what is helpful
> for building others up according to their needs
> that it may benefit those who listen."[6]

IF YOU MANAGE PAID STAFF, PLEASE STOP HERE
Read PAGE 229 before proceeding.
Thank You!

Are you a natural encourager? If you are, you already appreciate the value of your gift. You instinctively know that Volunteers need to know when they are doing a good job, when they are contributing positively to a cause they hold dear. The key reason they are there in the first place—is to make a difference. What you may not know is why most of our "encouragement" falls on unbelieving ears—and what you and I can do about it.

Whether you are a natural encourager or not, God commands us to "encourage one another daily."[7] Not just once in a while—every day. The Bible exhorts us to be encouragers more than 100 times in the New Testament alone! "Let us consider how we may spur one another toward love and good deeds." "Do not withhold good from those who deserve it, when it is in your power to act." "Remember, man does not live on bread alone, sometimes he needs

---

[6] Ephesians 4:29, NIV
[7] Hebrews 3:13, NIV

a little buttering up."[8]

How effective is our encouragement? Are we hitting the target? Few are surprised when secular bosses do a poor job of praising and encouraging. What surprises us is that churches, even with a Godly mandate, are not much better. Why is that?

Think of some of the compliments you have received in the past. Have you ever rejected one? Me, too. The question is why? I have observed that there are at least eight different reasons why compliments regularly fail to reach the heart and mind. You may have experienced some of them yourself.

WHY COMPLIMENTS MAY FAIL

1. PERCEIVED INSINCERITY

Do not fake it; it seldom works. That is why Hollywood pays George Clooney and Jennifer Lawrence millions of dollars—acting is not easy and people usually see through faked sincerity. It may be unfair, but you can actually be sincere and not get credit for it. How does that happen? Your body language and behavior can easily be misinterpreted.

For example:

- Voice: flat, unemotional, bored-sounding—perceived as insincere.

- Little Eye Contact: perceived as lying.

- Speed of Delivery: too fast ("I've got better places to go and better things to do."); too slow—sarcastic or condescending.

---

[8] John C. Maxwell, internationally known Christian leadership expert, speaker, and author.

SECRET #2: *Encourage with Credibility When Things Go Right*

2. LACK OF KNOWLEDGE OR PERCEIVED LACK OF KNOWLEDGE

If you say, "Great job! I appreciate all you do", they may be thinking, "What are you thanking me for? Did you even know what was involved?" To have credibility, you have to know what your Volunteers actually did and then communicate it to them in a way that they know, without a doubt, that you know. Be specific.

3. TOO DRAMATIC!!!

Some people always seem to need to talk in EXCLAMATION POINTS!! They talk as if everything from the largest to the smallest is "THE BEST!!", "AWESOME!!", "FANTASTIC!!", or "The way you photocopied those papers was phenomenal! You are amazing!"

4. MANIPULATIVE

You are rightly or wrongly credited with having an ulterior motive. They think: "You don't really mean what you say. You are just trying to get me to do more—or not quit."

Of course you want them to do more, and you definitely do not want them to quit. However, base your compliment on genuine appreciation for what they have done—not what they might do in the future.

They might also be thinking, "Why are you complimenting me? This isn't like you. What's really going on?" How do you overcome this kind of skepticism? The answer is counter-intuitive. Do it more rather than less. If it looks out of character for you, make a commitment to incorporate it into your character. Then it will not be out of place and you will sound credible.

5. REPETITION

"Great job, Sue!" "Great job, Bob!" "Great job, Phil!" And for variety, "Chris, great job!" Do people call you, *Johnny One-Note* behind your back? Do you say the same thing to everyone? How can anyone feel special if everyone else receives exactly the same compliment, no matter how much or how little they have done? Other frequent offenders: "Awesome!", "Way to go!" and the non-verbal thumbs up sign. Any one of these could be effective as long as it is not the only note in your tune.

6. YOU ARE PERCEIVED AS "FISHING FOR COMPLIMENTS"

It is natural and appropriate to give a compliment to someone with whom you have worked side-by-side on a project. Unfortunately, it has a built-in failure factor if it is not done well. When you tell them they have done a great job, they may interpret your comment as an attempt to manipulate them into telling you how wonderful you are. "Sue, I know you worked so hard on this ministry fair." (*Hint, hint...I worked hard, too, don't you think?*) This may be the farthest thing from your mind, but if it is in theirs, your compliment bites the dust when you grudgingly receive a compliment in return.

7. THE ANTI-SPOTLIGHT PERSON

Know who they are. Praise them in private or, even better; consider writing a personal note instead. Neglect is not the best option.

8. "NO BIG DEAL" RECIPIENT

No matter what you say or how you say it, this Volunteer will not accept the gift of a compliment. They de-value their actions as nothing worthy of praise or they de-value themselves. "Oh no, I didn't do anything special." Or "The others really did it all." Your opinion does not match their opinion and therefore is not valid. The rejection has little to do with you, your sincerity or your knowledge of their contribution. Your opinion simply does not count <u>at this time</u>. Do not give up on them. Continue to express your genuine

SECRET #2: *Encourage with Credibility When Things Go Right*

appreciation when it is appropriate. Their negative response is not a measure of your positive impact. You never know what might ultimately seep through the cracks in their armor. Pray for them that God's love will ultimately break through the armor that guards their heart.

Whether it is 8 or 88 reasons that our compliments fail, the sad truth is that many of our attempts fall short of the success to which God calls us. When He said to "encourage one another daily,"[9] I do not think we are stretching things too much to assume that He meant for us to be successful. He did not say, "Give it the old college try and let the chips fall where they may." By putting a little effort into it, doing our homework and making sure the right pieces are in place, our compliments can be the gifts we meant them to be.

How do we do that? The good news is there is a way and it does not even come close to being as difficult as brain surgery. Everyone can do it.

THE HOME RUN COMPLIMENT

Let's take a look at a **Home Run Compliment** that will help us achieve the goal that God set before us. In the game of baseball, we have to touch all four bases to get a **Home Run**. Since most of the reasons people reject compliments hang out at **First Base**, getting past **First** is more than half the battle.

I regularly teach a workshop called *Encouragement and Recognition* which teaches this specific skill to church leaders and Volunteer team leaders. Following the workshop, it is common to hear participants say, "I can't believe that 90% of my compliments are **First Base** compliments!" It is pretty clear, if you intend to be an excellent encourager, you have to successfully get past **First**.

---

[9] Hebrews 3:13, NIV

The **Home Run Compliment** has four parts. When all four are present, we stand the greatest chance of success. Even though there is never a 100% guarantee, we will have done everything we can to package our gift in a way to be positively received.

Take a quick look at all compliments in general—Nouns, Adjectives and Verbs. (See diagram below.)

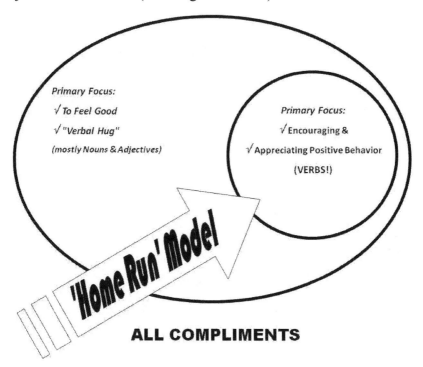

ALL COMPLIMENTS

All compliments are positive—at least in theory. Most compliments focus on some admirable trait or characteristic. It is equivalent to a *verbal hug.*

"You have a lovely smile." "You have a great way with kids." "You are a wonderful helper." "You are the best teacher."

At the risk of sounding like your freshman English teacher, let me draw your attention to the words. You will notice that most compliments are primarily adjectives (lovely/great/wonderful/best) and nouns (smile/way/helper/teacher). Don't get me wrong. They

SECRET #2: *Encourage with Credibility When Things Go Right*

are better than a poke-in-the-eye, but they are also more likely to be rejected as vague, manipulative, or overly dramatic.

The compliment that has the best chance of being received is the one that zeroes in on behavior. That means you have to use verbs. What did the person actually do? Of course, it helps if you have done your homework and actually know what your Volunteer has done.

The good news is that most vague, adjective-loaded compliments can be turned into **Home Run Compliments** by answering one simple question. "What behavior did the person exhibit to earn the label *wonderful helper, best teacher* or *great way with kids*?"

It is more meaningful and believable to say, "Thank you for being a wonderful helper. Every time I call, even at the last minute, you always come through for me." Just saying "You're great!" is more likely to hit the trash than the target.

Hit a **Home Run** with a 4–Part Compliment for Positive Behavior.

A Statement of Thanks/Appreciation or Quality

1st
BASE

- "Thanks"
- "I appreciate…"
- "Great job!"
- "Way to go!"
- "I admire…"

Using three at the same time ("Thanks a lot. That was a great job. I really appreciate what you've done.") does not make it a **Home Run**. You have just gotten to **First Base** three times!

2nd BASE

A Behavior Specific Statement

- "Thanks for <u>helping me set up</u> this morning."

- "Excellent job <u>organizing the storage area</u>."

- "I really appreciate <u>your attention to detail and follow-through</u>. When you <u>say you will get something done, it is as good as done</u>."

(Note: You have the potential here for a **Grand Slam**: one compliment with two or more specific behaviors that you appreciate—i.e., <u>thoroughness</u> and <u>reliability</u>).

3rd BASE

A Positive Impact Statement

The specific behavior you mentioned at second base was important because it had a positive impact to:

- Your organization's goals/morale/achievement
- Other people or their goals
- Kingdom goals
- You or your goals

  Examples:
  - "I appreciate your warm smile. <u>It really makes me feel welcome here</u>."
  - "Your singing is amazing. <u>You really reach people and touch them in a very special way</u>."
  - "Excellent job organizing the storage

area. <u>Now we can find what we need quickly</u>."

- "I really appreciate your attention to detail and follow-through. When you say you'll get something done, it is as good as done! I shudder to think <u>what might have happened if you had not gotten all those permission slips in time</u>. Thanks."

Please Note: This last positive impact is actually a negative that would have happened if they had not done such an excellent job. Many ministry jobs that Volunteers perform fall into this category (e.g., parking and traffic workers—if they do their jobs well, no one notices; if they do their jobs poorly, fender-benders, traffic jams and ugliness occur). Be creative when looking for positive impacts. Do not forget to consider what might have happened if your Volunteers had not done their jobs well.

Deliver with Sincerity from the Heart

Finally, to truly hit a **Home Run**, everything must be delivered with sincerity. George Burns once said that "Sincerity is the key to success. Once you can fake that, you've got it made!" While I heartily agree that sincerity is the key to success, we are looking for the real deal. But remember sincerity alone is not enough. **First, Second** and **Third Base** make your compliment credible.

8½ SECRETS

"Feeling gratitude and not expressing it is like wrapping a present and not giving it."[10] Encouragement is a gift we give to each other, but it does not become a gift until the other person actually accepts it. Credibility is critical to the process.

> *"Feeling gratitude and not expressing it is like wrapping a present and not giving it."*
> *− William Arthur Ward*

The **Home Run Compliment** may seem like a lot of effort just to recognize a Volunteer's behavior. So, why bother? Consider:

- How important to your organization is the work your Volunteers do? In most churches, even the smaller ones, Volunteers typically provide thousands of man-hours of work each year. Could you do without them?

- Would you like to have more Volunteers? Keep in mind that *Volunteers walk and talk*. If you are lax about expressing your genuine appreciation, it may not be a surprise to them why you have difficulty recruiting new Volunteers.

- Oh yeah, God said…

The Home Run Compliment is simple, easy and effective. The good news—it becomes second nature very quickly. NIKE said, "Just Do It." God said the same thing—only first: "Do not withhold

---

[10] William Arthur Ward, (1921-1994) one of America's most quoted writers of inspirational maxims and author of *Fountains of Faith*.

SECRET #2: *Encourage with Credibility When Things Go Right*

good from those who deserve it when it is in your power to act",[11] "Encourage one another daily"[12] and, not surprisingly, "whoever refreshes others will be refreshed."[13] Isn't that just like God? He turns around and gives us the same blessing we have given to another!

*"Too often we underestimate the power
of a touch, a smile, a kind word, a listening ear,
an honest compliment, or the smallest act of caring,
all of which have the potential to turn a life around."*[14]
— Leo Buscaglia

---

[11] Proverbs 3:27, NIV
[12] Hebrews 3:13, NIV
[13] Proverbs 11:25b, NIV
[14] Leo F. Buscaglia, PhD (1924 –1998), American Author, Motivational Speaker, professor.

☑ Action Steps for Encouragement:

☐ 1. Make a list that includes each member of your family and at least two Volunteers or friends that deserve to be recognized or appreciated. See **Appendix 2A Worksheet**.

☐ 2. Write a **Home Run Compliment** for each. See **Appendices 2B and 2C Worksheets.**

- Remember to make it behavior specific and simple. Hopefully, you are not trying to write a compliment to cover the last 10 years of drought. (This has happened!) Stick to one event/action/behavior to focus on for each compliment.

- Use everyday language. You are not writing a Hallmark greeting card. It does not have to rhyme or be full of flowery words. In fact, it is better if it is not. Who actually talks like that, anyway?

- Please deliver your family compliments at a rate of *only one per day*. If you deliver them all at once, credibility is seriously at risk. "Who are you and what have you done with my real mother/father/wife/husband…?"

- Extra benefit: The **Home Run Compliment** can easily be adapted to create a great thank you note. (Remember that ANTI-SPOTLIGHT Volunteer.)

☐ 3. Go to www.JuneKenny.com for free training Worksheets and helpful tips on working with Volunteers.

"When you inspire others, you inspire yourself."
– Anonymous (but very wise person)

SECRET #2: *Encourage with Credibility When Things Go Right*

☑ Actions I Plan to Take to Encourage Others:

1. _____

2. _____

3. _____

4. _____

5. _____

6. _____

7. _____

8. _____

*"Kind words can be short and easy to speak,
but their echoes are truly endless."*
— *Mother Teresa*

APPENDIX 2A: *Who Needs Encouragement? WORKSHEET*

Who needs/deserves encouragement in your sphere of influence? (Be sure to include family members.)

☐ 1.

☐ 2.

☐ 3.

☐ 4.

☐ 5.

☐ 6.

☐ 7.

☐ 8.

☐ 9.

☐ 10.

Write a **Home Run Compliment** for each so you can be *intentionally* spontaneous when you see them next.
See **Appendix 2C Worksheet.**

APPENDIX 2B: *Expressing Yourself Accurately*

Expressing Yourself Accurately

Getting to 1st Base:
A Statement of Thanks/Appreciation or Quality

Words that express <u>Thanks</u> or <u>Appreciation</u>:

I appreciate…	I'm proud…	I'm grateful for…
I respect…	Thanks/Thank You	Bless you for…
I admire…	I love the way you…	I treasure….
I noticed…	I'm amazed…	I've observed…
and others…		

Words that express <u>Quality</u> (usually adjectives or nouns):

great job	awesome	way to go!
talented	gifted	angelic
wonderful	sweet	admirable
sensational	brilliant	inspirational
accomplished	experienced	masterful
qualified	the best	an expert
beautiful	creative	amazing
delicious	tasty	yummy
incredible	miraculous	fantastic
superb	you're too much	terrific
stunning	clever	fabulous
cool	magnificent	something else
exceptional	unusual	unique
colorful	cute	enjoyable
outstanding	proficient	memorable
striking	a Rock Star!	
and others…		

49

APPENDIX 2B: Expressing Yourself Accurately

Getting to 2nd Base:
A Behavior Specific Statement

What <u>Specific Behavior</u> are you thanking, appreciating or recognizing them for? Your compliment will be much more meaningful (and believable) if you are accurate and precise in your description. This is what builds your credibility.

Getting to 3rd Base:
A Positive Impact Statement

This statement answers the question: Why is this specific behavior important to you? Why is this behavior worthy of comment?

Example:

"Thank you so much for staying after the meeting to help me clean up. It really meant a lot to me because:

- …<u>it allowed me to get done quickly so I could get home before the kids went to bed.</u>"
- …<u>it offered me much needed help after an exhausting day.</u>"
- …<u>it provided me with pleasant company to make the job more fun.</u>"
- …<u>we were unexpectedly short-handed tonight.</u>"
- …and others

APPENDIX 2C: *Home Run Compliment WORKSHEET*

Hit a Home Run with a 4–Part Compliment for Positive Behavior

1st BASE

A Statement of Thanks/Appreciation or Quality

_____

_____

_____

2nd BASE

A Behavior Specific Statement

_____

_____

_____

3rd BASE

A Positive Impact Statement

_____

_____

_____

HOME RUN

Deliver with Sincerity from the Heart

51

#3: Give Compassionate Criticism When Things Go Wrong—

You Owe it to Your Volunteers to Tell Them

So, how do we do that?

Do you know leaders who are thrilled to have to correct another adult's behavior? I don't. Do you know anyone who enjoys hearing that they have failed or done something incorrectly? I don't. Why is criticism so difficult to do well and receive well?

For some reason handling criticism is especially awkward in ministry. The reasons I have heard are many. "I don't want to hurt her feelings." "If I say anything, she may quit." "I'm uncomfortable being critical." "There is no good way to do this, so it doesn't matter how I say it." "I get so frustrated with the Volunteer (or the situation) that the easiest thing to do is to get rid of him and make the problem go away." "I'm too busy. It takes too much time." Do any of these sound familiar to you?

Over the last decade, I have observed hundreds of Ministry Leaders in action. Many are working with Volunteers in effective and loving ways achieving excellent results – even when correcting behavior. Unfortunately, a few are figuratively leaving dead bodies in their wake. In ministry, this is a tragedy of epic proportion. You probably know who I am talking about. In truth, so does everyone else.

Is it really easier or more effective in the long run to make avoidance your leadership strategy of choice? Consider investing the time to coach them to success instead. I will concede that avoidance is easier in the short term. However, being constantly frustrated by poor performance or dealing with an endless supply of newbies can't be any fun either.

Current data suggests that to replace a corporate employee with a new one costs the company more than that employee's annual salary. Costs are attributed to lost productivity, finding a replacement, new employee training, learning curve, etc. While the annual salary of the Volunteer is zero, their dollars and cents contribution to your ministry is priceless. If paid staff had to cover their workload, both money and valuable time would be expended or the job would go undone. Respecting Volunteers as if they were paid staff would help set the tone that Volunteers are fully-engaged partners in your ministry. Removing obstacles to success and providing tools to enhance performance is *Job #1* for the Ministry Leader. Simply replacing a Volunteer with another beginner does not save time, money or eliminate the recurring problem of poor performance—particularly when avoidance is your strategy of choice.

Fortunately, the Bible has given us clear directives about the importance of coaching each other to stay on track and do our best. We are to be appreciative when others coach us—even if we do not particularly like it at the time—and to be gracious to others when we coach them. "A gentle answer turns away wrath, but harsh words stir up anger."[15]

What does God say about criticism? First, criticism should be treated like gold. We are told in the book of Proverbs that, "To one who listens, valid criticism is like a gold earring or other gold jewelry."[16] Proverbs also teaches, "Whoever loves discipline loves knowledge, but he who hates correction is stupid."[17] We are foolish if we do not appreciate the value of wise counsel. Could the Bible be more blunt?

A wise man once said, "The tongue is the only tool that gets

---

[15] Proverbs 15:1, NIV
[16] Proverbs 25:12, NLT
[17] Proverbs 12:1, NIV

SECRET #3: *Give Compassionate Criticism When Things Go Wrong*

sharper with use."[18] How true. I am fairly certain Washington Irving did not mean *more refined* by the word sharp.

Proverbs—the Book of Wisdom—has over 150 specific verses to address what we say and how we say it. I think it is safe to say that God cares about how we communicate with each other. God is calling us as believers to help one another succeed. So, the question is not *if* but *how*?

If you start with the following assumption, you will be halfway home—not to mention that it happens to be the truth: **Volunteers want to make a positive difference. They want to succeed.** No one volunteers with the intention of failing.

> *Volunteers want to make a positive difference. They want to succeed.*

Of course, being human, Volunteers also may want other things as well (e.g., a sense of importance, power, opportunities to use favored talents or skills, friendship, community, etc.). But making a positive difference is at the core of why Volunteers volunteer. Even if you do not feel your particular Volunteer is interested in doing a good job, it is in your best interest to treat them *as if* that were true. Adopting an *as if* approach is worth its weight in gold.

Why is the *as if* approach so important to a leader's effectiveness? It is important because it will help you keep your cool at all times—which is critical. The very hint of criticism can elicit defensiveness in just about anyone. They will quit listening and become defensive. Someone has to be in control of the situation and, unfortunately, the job falls to you—the Ministry Leader. If your emotions are not completely under control, no

---

[18] Washington Irving, (1783-1859), American Author and Diplomat.

one's will be.

A critical task for you as a leader is to find ways to help your Volunteers succeed. You have day-to-day ministry objectives to think about, but your Volunteers' spiritual development is also a key factor to consider. You are providing the opportunity for them to experience the fullness of God's blessings and grow closer to Him as they engage in His work. This is not the lesser goal—it may even be the most important one.

You are providing the opportunity for them to experience the fullness of God's blessings and grow closer to Him as they engage in His work. This is not the lesser goal— it may even be the most important one.

Giving an effective compliment is important. Giving effective criticism is even more important—and can be much trickier. If not done well, it is likely to make matters worse rather than better. Planning ahead and thinking through exactly what you will say is extremely important. But what exactly do you say? And how do you say it?

The good news is that you can successfully redirect a Volunteer's unwanted, inappropriate or ineffective behavior— when you deliver it with a heart. **Compassionate Criticism** is about helping someone get back on track to make a positive impact. If you remember that your goal is to help them succeed, it will go a long way toward increasing your comfort level as well. **Compassionate Criticism** works because it is respectful, persuasive and puts both you and your Volunteer at ease. (Well, at least more at ease.)

SECRET #3: *Give Compassionate Criticism When Things Go Wrong*

COMPASSIONATE CRITICISM: TWO VERSIONS

The Anybody Model can be used with anyone or anytime but the more powerful **For Friends Only Model** can only be used with people who love you. For success, using either version, we must see our relationship as adult-to-adult. Adult-to-adult is key. Too often leaders, supervisors or bosses—even in ministry—assume that authority over someone's work behavior gives them permission to engage in a parent-child relationship with another adult. This assumption always leads to disaster (sometimes sooner, sometimes later, but ALWAYS). Compassionate Criticism helps you maintain an adult-to-adult conversation even when the temptation may be to revert to teacher-student or parent-child. Unless your Volunteer actually is your own child (and under the age of 16), it is NEVER appropriate to assume a parent-child communication approach when giving criticism to another adult.

Any time you need to criticize anyone's behavior, pray about it and plan ahead so that you are in complete control of your attitude, your emotions and your words. This can be a touchy situation; this is not the time for spontaneity.

If you tend toward introversion, you probably automatically think through what you plan to say before you say it. It is one of the blessings that God gives to introverts. If, however, you are more extroverted, like me, thinking before you speak takes considerably more effort. Extroverts tend to *wing it* and say whatever comes into their minds—then tweak and adjust as they go. If you are more extroverted, this is definitely the time to fight that natural urge. Giving criticism calls for us to be super-prepared to make sure we are conveying exactly the message in exactly the right way to maximize our success with this person.

Let's get started. When I said you need to have a heart to do criticism well, I meant it quite literally. The letters of A. H.E.A.R.T. will help you remember all the essential steps to

8½ SECRETS

Compassionate Criticism when you are face-to-face in that stressful situation.

A. H.E.A.R.T.

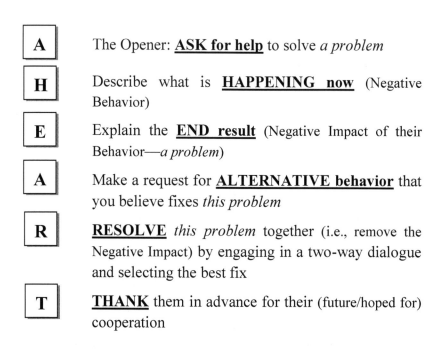

A	The Opener: **ASK for help** to solve *a problem*
H	Describe what is **HAPPENING now** (Negative Behavior)
E	Explain the **END result** (Negative Impact of their Behavior—*a problem*)
A	Make a request for **ALTERNATIVE behavior** that you believe fixes *this problem*
R	**RESOLVE** *this problem* together (i.e., remove the Negative Impact) by engaging in a two-way dialogue and selecting the best fix
T	**THANK** them in advance for their (future/hoped for) cooperation

Before we are ready to criticize anyone, compassionately or otherwise, a little homework is in order—get our *ducks in a row*, so to speak. An important first step is to take time to clarify in your own mind what exactly is **Happening now** that is creating a problem for you. Ask yourself: "What is this Volunteer *doing* that throws a monkey wrench into our goals?" "What are they *doing* that is making our job harder?" "What would I like to ask them to stop *doing*?" "What is the Volunteer *not doing* that I would like them to do?" Please note that *doing* is the key. It is behavior that is somehow creating the problem.

This behavior must be described clearly and accurately, followed by the negative **End result** caused by that behavior. The

SECRET #3: *Give Compassionate Criticism When Things Go Wrong*

negative **End result** is the real problem you want to fix. It becomes your most powerful persuader. Through this process the Volunteer is made aware (maybe for the first time) of the need to change something in order to be successful. Remember your leadership promise? Treat Volunteers *as if* they want to make a positive difference. Because they do.

I know it sounds obvious, but it is a little trickier than it seems. It is so easy to draw negative conclusions about people from their behavior without even realizing it. Unfortunately, when we do this, we tend to articulate our conclusions instead of sticking with the objective observed behavior. For example: When someone arrives late for a meeting, we may conclude that he is *irresponsible*. The objective behavior is actually *arriving 10 minutes late*, not irresponsibility. Irresponsibility was our conclusion – the label we attached to the behavior. Perhaps he was late due to the necessity of handling team, church or family business or an unavoidable traffic jam which legitimately delayed his arrival. We do not know.

"But it is true! They are irresponsible! They are always late!" Okay, I believe you. They are always late. Guess what? It doesn't matter—at this moment. At this moment, you want to change their future behavior—not beat them up about their past failures. This is a new day, a new event, and you are deciding to handle it in a new and more effective way. Creating guilt, shame or defensiveness is not a great start to winning future cooperation from anyone. Your job as a leader is to help your Volunteers become more competent in their and your ministry.

Here are a couple of non-productive examples of criticism I have heard more than once. Have you heard them before or maybe even used them? Here is a mini-challenge: How might you intentionally reduce the negative impact of these statements?

- **"You are irresponsible. I can't count on you."**
  Why not use a more accurate statement instead? "When you showed up 30 minutes late today, it left me short-handed and we had to rush to get the job done."

- **"You're not doing that right. Do it the correct way."**
  Your Volunteer translates this statement into, "You are not doing it MY WAY." The statement has a number of problems. It is too vague. Since there was no explanation of how doing it their way prevented the goal from being achieved, you are likely to be viewed as arbitrarily controlling. Their way may not be your way, but that does not necessarily make it a bad choice. An alternative statement might be "You may not have realized it, but when you do XYZ, it creates this problem for _____. I would appreciate if you could do ABC next time." Note: this assumes you have been able to identify an objective negative **End result**—not just your personal preference.

THE *AS IF* APPROACH

Even if it is true that "they always _____", it may help if you remember the *as if* approach again. Act *as if* this is the first time this behavior has occurred. The *as if* approach will help you keep your frustration level manageable while you calmly explain why this behavior creates a problem (i.e., a negative **End result**) for you or your team.

If you typically wait until molehills have become mountains before taking corrective action, the term *gunnysacking* may apply to you. Do you save up every transgression until you have hit your limit? Then, do you dump the whole bag at once? The other person is often blindsided and surprised that anything is wrong. They may think that you have suddenly had a nervous breakdown. "After all,

SECRET #3: *Give Compassionate Criticism When Things Go Wrong*

this didn't bother you the last fifty times I did it. You never said anything before."

It is hard enough to keep from being frustrated or disappointed when a Volunteer you counted on fails to perform as expected. Adding their previous transgressions to your current disappointment is not going to help you calmly deal with today's situation. Besides, you could have dealt with the previous incidents long ago—when they first occurred. Saving them up until now was a choice you (or a previous leader) made—not the greatest choice, but a choice nonetheless. New choices can be made. Hooray! That is what change is all about.

As Christ followers, we get a new chance each day to do things better. In fact, that is one of the blessings we have received through God's grace! We have received the ultimate *life do-over*. As leaders, we now have endless opportunities, on a smaller scale, to live in this Christ-mode with others. So today, we focus only on what happened today and how this specific behavior negatively impacted the meeting, the team, me, our goals, etc. Staying calm, staying in the moment and sticking with the facts will help us approach a touchy situation with the grace and dignity both we and our Volunteers deserve.

Criticism is definitely about telling the truth, but it is not necessarily about telling the brutal truth. Remember the goal—you want to change future behavior, not create more reasons to resist change. Being truthful does not necessarily require sharing every thought or annoyance that goes through your head. Thank goodness!

Yes, share the truthful thoughts about their <u>exact behavior</u> and its <u>negative impact</u> on you or your goals. This truth encourages their cooperation to change. Withhold (please!) those thoughts that create defensiveness, guilt and shame (e.g., "you are unprofessional, lazy and gross me out"). Remember:

- "A gentle answer turns away wrath, but harsh words stir

61

up anger."[19]
- "Pleasant words are a honeycomb, sweet to the soul and healing to the bones."[20]
- "The real art of conversation is not only to say the right thing in the right place but to leave unsaid the wrong thing at the tempting moment."[21]

The bottom line is that defensive people do not cooperate. Shamed individuals can frequently become passive-aggressive antagonists to you and your ministry. Who needs that?

Your goal is to bring about a change in behavior in a way that allows the Volunteer to be successful, while keeping everyone's dignity intact. When you ask people to change their behavior, it is important to give them the reason why the change is needed. Explaining the real problem—which is the negative **End result** of their specific behavior—goes a long way in providing that compelling reason. Telling them "I don't like what you are doing because it is not the way I would do it" may sound persuasive to you. I can guarantee that it is much less compelling to your Volunteer.

THE ANYBODY MODEL

Take a closer look at **The Anybody Model** which is your *go-to* safest choice. You do not have to have an on-going or long-standing relationship in place. You will find this is a gracious way to explain to anyone, in almost any circumstance, how their behavior is creating a problem. Then ask for their help by altering that behavior in a specific way. If you deliver this request in a non-accusatory, calm and respectful manner, you will have a great chance at winning their cooperation.

---

[19] Proverbs 15:1, NIV
[20] Proverbs 16:24, NIV
[21] Lady Dorothy Nevill, 1826-1913, English writer.

SECRET #3: *Give Compassionate Criticism When Things Go Wrong*

There are six steps to **The Anybody Model**. <u>Each step</u> is included for a reason and important for success. **The Anybody Model** includes three motivators – identified with a ♥. I define a motivator as "a compelling reason for another adult to want to change his behavior."

You are hoping to achieve willing cooperation – not compliance when you are looking and sabotage when you are not. Your goal is to help your Volunteers succeed and experience God's blessings, not blindly yield to your authority.

This communication model is effective for a number of reasons. One, it clearly states who owns the problem, i.e., the person bothered by what is **<u>Happening now</u>**. Please note: this means you—not them. They think things are working just fine or at least no harm, no foul. They are going to need a compelling reason or two to think it necessary to change their behavior.

The three primary motivators in this model are:

1) the negative **<u>End result</u>** of their current behavior

2) their natural desire to be helpful

3) your sincere expression of gratitude

Remember: it is important that your delivery be adult-to-adult, non-accusatory, non-threatening and delivered using your special *butter voice*. You know the one I mean—the one you use at Thanksgiving when the hot rolls pass your way. "Could you please pass the butter?" It works every time at Thanksgiving. It is your best bet here, too.

> *Remember: it is important that your delivery be adult-to-adult, non-accusatory, non-threatening and delivered using your special butter voice.*

THE ANYBODY MODEL: HAVE A. H.E.A.R.T.

THE SIX STEPS ARE: (♥ ♥ ♥ Motivators)

A	1.	♥ The Opener: **ASK for help** to solve *a problem*
H	2.	Describe what is **HAPPENING now** (Negative Behavior)
E	3.	♥ Explain the **END result** (Negative Impact of their Behavior—*a problem*)
A	4.	Make a request for **ALTERNATIVE behavior** that you believe fixes *this problem*
R	5.	**RESOLVE** *this problem* together (i.e., remove the Negative Impact) by engaging in a two-way dialogue and selecting the best fix
T	6.	♥ **THANK** them in advance for their *(future/hoped for)* cooperation

SECRET #3: *Give Compassionate Criticism When Things Go Wrong*

Let's take a closer look at each step and how it works.

| A | **STEP ONE:** ♥ **The Opener:** <u>**ASK for help**</u> **to solve** *a problem*

Every conversation has to begin in some fashion. I recommend starting with a motivational opener. "Can I talk with you for a minute? I have a problem I could use your help with." This gets your Volunteer's attention to let them know that you want to talk and it taps into a motivator that triggers positive behavior in many of us—the desire to help others. This opening statement achieves three important goals:

- You have a reasonable, non-threatening and effective way to start a difficult conversation.

- You acknowledge who owns the problem. You do. "I have a problem…." Remember they do not have a problem with the status quo. They are either oblivious to or discount the severity of the problem. While they may know that their behavior is not ideal, to them it is not a big deal. It is important for you to recognize and accept this fact so you can maintain your calm, cool and collected demeanor.

- You are providing a possible motivator for them to change their behavior (i.e., the desire to help someone else).

Of course, not everyone in the world is motivated by the thought of helping others. However, many are. Why not act *as if*? What have you got to lose? It may just work. You are more likely to win the cooperation of your Volunteers when you invite them to help you solve a problem and follow up with a logical case for why their current behavior is not working.

| H | **STEP TWO: Describe what is <u>HAPPENING now</u> (i.e., Negative Behavior)**

Describe the observed negative behavior in a non-accusatory tone of voice using objective terms. By objective, I mean exactly what you have seen or heard—no elaboration needed. This is not the time for exaggeration or derogatory labels.

Do you hear a difference in the following? "I overheard you and Sue *arguing* in the hallway a few minutes ago" versus "I overheard you and Sue *talking loudly* in the hallway a few minutes ago." The first draws a conclusion about the meaning of the behavior ("arguing"); the other simply describes what was observed. Objectivity is not only safer ground to tread, it is more effective to stick with what you see or hear.

You can express the behavior you have observed in two different ways: the active voice or the passive voice.

Active Voice: "you do XYZ"
Passive Voice: "XYZ occurs"

If you are concerned that the Volunteer might become overly emotional or the relationship is too fragile to risk, I recommend using the passive voice. It tends to soften the message delivery without losing clarity. It usually takes a little more thought and *wordsmithing* to get it into the passive voice format.

Active voice (Newsletter Editor to Article Contributor): "*When you give me your article after the deadline*, it really puts me in a bind to get the newsletter done in time for mailing." Passive voice: "*When articles are turned in late*, it really puts me in a bind to get the newsletter done in time for mailing." Clarity is still intact because you both know whose article is being discussed. The difference? The delivery sounds less accusatory.

I often hear people minimizing the poor performance or describing it in such vague terms in order to soften the blow of a negative message. This just makes the message unintelligible. To

SECRET #3: *Give Compassionate Criticism When Things Go Wrong*

be effective, your message must have unequivocal clarity and still be respectful and even kind. **Compassionate Criticism** does that.

Whether you use the passive or active voice, the message is always best delivered privately to each person who exhibited the behavior you are trying to modify. One of the things that drives team members crazy, both in the corporate world and in ministry, is for a wimpy leader to try to correct one person's behavior by lecturing the entire team as though all were offenders. It is hard enough to be corrected for your own errors. No one appreciates being corrected for someone else's.

For some reason in our culture, when the word *you* is used as the subject of a sentence containing criticism ("You did XYZ" or "You didn't do ABC"), it feels like an index finger wagging in our faces. The likelihood of instant defensiveness is high and is counterproductive to our goal of winning cooperation. Tone of voice plays an important role, too. Think, *butter voice.* But even when your tone of voice is pleasant, your Volunteer still may hear condemnation in spite of your best intentions.

| E | **STEP THREE:** ♥ **Explain the END result (Negative Impact of their Behavior—***a problem***)**

This is, without question, the most important motivator you have in **The Anybody Model.** Believe it or not, most people have no clue that their behavior is causing problems for anyone. They are simply trying to get through life as best they can...usually with blinders on to the rest of the world. Observe other drivers on any given day, on any freeway, in any city—you will be quickly convinced. If more people had *other-awareness* or could grasp the concept of *collateral damage,* we would have a lot less need to deliver criticism—compassionate or otherwise. Most people seem genuinely surprised to learn that their behavior has created a problem for someone else. They often willingly alter their behavior once they learn it had an unintended negative impact (i.e. *collateral* *damage*) on others.

By "Negative impact" we are referring to a naturally-occurring and obvious consequence of their behavior. Suppose a Volunteer

> *If more people had* other-awareness *or could grasp the concept of* collateral damage, *we would have a lot less need to deliver criticism—compassionate or otherwise.*

signed up to provide dessert for a luncheon and then failed to do so. What might you say? "When you agreed to provide a dessert for the luncheon and then didn't call to let us know that you couldn't, we ended up short a dessert with no time to fix the problem." What could you say to a Volunteer who is consistently late to a team meeting? Try this on for size. "Coming in late causes you to miss important information. Then, when we take time to review, it extends the meeting which is not fair to your team members. If we do not take the time, you would be operating with only partial information."

Your disappointment or hurt feelings are not objective consequences. They are arbitrarily-imposed consequences and tend to be weak persuaders to others. Your feelings have no useful place in **The Anybody Model.** However, they may be effective motivators when using the **For Friends Only Model**—assuming that the person actually cares about your feelings. Even then, feelings never replace the negative **END result.** In fact, the negative **END result** is the most persuasive part of your argument.

It is so important that if you cannot think of anything except "I don't like it," you have no business criticizing the person for their behavior. If the behavior is important enough to eliminate, it should be causing some identifiable problem to someone or something. Do your homework. Ask yourself: "Why is this behavior so bad?" If

SECRET #3: *Give Compassionate Criticism When Things Go Wrong*

you have a good answer to this question, you are half-way home.

Clearly explaining the **negative END result** is critical. It is crucial that you define it accurately because it is the problem your Volunteer is going to try to help you solve. One class participant

*...the negative **END result** is the most persuasive part of your argument.*

illustrates what I mean by "defining the real problem." She initially identified Step 2 (the unwanted behavior) as "When you leave your folded clothes in the laundry area..." and Step 3 (the negative impact) as "...they get in disarray as you go in and look for a shirt to wear each day."

It is true the shirts may be a mess, but how has she shown this is a problem for her? With the problem defined in this way, his response will predictably be "No problem, honey, I don't care if they're messed up. I can still find what I need."

I asked her if she liked that answer. She didn't.

Her real problem was space. His clothes took up all the laundry room counter tops. It was difficult for her to do other loads of laundry because there was no place to fold the clothes.

Once the class participant substituted her real problem as the negative impact, her husband would be more inclined to work on the "I need more space" problem rather than her "I'm bugged by your clutter" problem. If you are precise about what your problem is, you just might get it fixed.

If you are precise about what your problem is, you just might get it fixed.

A | **STEP FOUR: Make a request for <u>ALTERNATIVE BEHAVIOR</u> that you believe fixes *this problem***

State the desired behavior you would appreciate seeing instead:

- "I would appreciate it if you could...."
- "Could you help me out by...?"
- "Would it be possible for you to...?"
- "Would you mind...?"
- "I need for you to...."

R | **STEP FIVE: <u>RESOLVE</u> *this problem* together (i.e., remove the negative impact) by engaging in a two-way dialogue and selecting the best fix**

Ask for their input:

- "What do you think? Would this be possible, plausible, doable...?"
- "Do you have any other ideas that might help or resolve this problem?" (In fact, you may actually get a better solution than the one you originally proposed. I have had this happen on many occasions.)

SECRET #3: *Give Compassionate Criticism When Things Go Wrong*

| T | **STEP SIX:** ♥ **THANK** them in advance for their (*future/hoped for*) **cooperation**

Thank your Volunteers for their cooperation and support—in advance! Genuine gratitude motivates. Remember you are the one with the problem and need their help.

- "Thanks so much for your help/understanding."
- "I really appreciate your assistance with this."
- "I appreciate whatever you can do to help me with this problem."

It is important to thank them in advance, especially when the person initially seems resistant or unlikely to be cooperative. Often when they have had a chance to think calmly about your request, they become more willing to comply.

The *For Friends Only* Model adds only one additional step, but it is an important one. **_Your feelings_** have the potential to make this the most effective request for change when used with people who care enough about you to be influenced by your feelings. Most people generally need a reason to change behavior. Combining four motivators (♥a desire to be helpful, ♥**your feelings**, ♥the negative impact of their behavior and ♥genuine gratitude) makes this statement the strongest request for cooperative behavior change.

THE SEVEN STEPS ARE: (♥♥♥♥ MOTIVATORS)

A	1. ♥ The Opener: **ASK for help** to solve *a problem*
+ *feelings*	2. ♥ Share **your feelings** (only if you are sure they care about them.)
H	3. Describe what is **HAPPENING now** (Negative Behavior)
E	4. ♥ Explain the **END result** (Negative Impact of their Behavior – *a problem*)
A	5. Make a request for **ALTERNATIVE behavior** that you believe fixes *this problem*
R	6. **RESOLVE** *this problem* together (i.e., remove the negative impact) by engaging in a two-way dialogue and selecting the best fix
T	7. ♥ **THANK** them in advance for their (*future/hoped for*) cooperation

Your feelings are a powerful addition which must be used carefully in order to be effective. It is important that you express your feelings honestly, but in an understated and self-controlled way: *frustrated vs. furious, confused vs. dumbfounded, disappointed vs. crushed, irritated vs. outraged*, etc. In other words, do not be overly dramatic. Try to remember how you might have felt the first time the behavior occurred before the accumulation began. Hopefully, you were somewhat calmer at that point. While you want to be absolutely clear and factual about describing the behavior, you will get better results if you do not overplay the feeling card.

SECRET #3: *Give Compassionate Criticism When Things Go Wrong*

EXAMPLE: "Julie, I have a problem I could use your help with. *I was frustrated* when I went looking for _____ the other day and couldn't find it. It turned up in another cabinet. I finally found it, but it took an extra 20 minutes that I didn't have that day. It would be terrific, when you are cleaning up next time at the end of your class, if you could put the _____ back in the instructors' cabinet so other teachers could find it more quickly. I appreciate whatever you can do to help us avoid this mix-up in the future. Thanks so much!" If you are unsure whether Julie cares about your *frustration*, simply omit the feeling statement and use **The Anybody Model** instead.

In summary, **Compassionate Criticism** is simply more successful. It gives us a way to tackle an important, usually awkward, often high-risk encounter with a fellow human being. We want it to turn out well. We want to be successful. We want them to be successful. This is our best shot given there are no silver bullets, no guarantees when it comes to human interaction—at least this side of heaven.

1. **This model is effective because it is:**

    Healthy – You are simply stating what needs to be done and why—without anger or accusation.

    Persuasive – It contains reasons (i.e., motivators) why they might want to change their behavior in order to be more successful.

    Respectful – Your demeanor is calm and supportive.

    Compassionate – Volunteers want to make a positive impact and you care enough about them to help them be successful.

2. It is effective because it contains three or four motivators:

- ♥ Desire to help
- ♥ Negative impact of current behavior
- ♥ Your feelings
- ♥ The power of sincere gratitude

3. It is effective because your tone of voice is not irritated or angry (i.e., *butter voice*).

4. It is effective because your word choice is not accusatory.
Behavior is stated neutrally in behavior-specific terms.

5. It is effective because its format conveys "we are not adversaries."
The problem (i.e., negative impact of current behavior) is stated neutrally and separate from you or me. I am not trying to fix you; you and I are partnering to fix it.

> *"Do not let any unwholesome talk come out
> of your mouths, but only what is helpful
> for building others up according to their needs,
> that it may benefit those who listen."*[22]

---

[22] Ephesians 4:29, NIV

SECRET #3: *Give Compassionate Criticism When Things Go Wrong*

☑ Action Steps for Compassionate Criticism:

☐ 1. Use the *as if* **approach** to leadership. It works!

☐ 2. Use **The Anybody Model** (♥♥♥) and the **For Friends Only Model** (♥♥♥♥) to help prepare for your next Volunteer feedback sessions. *Getting Volunteers back on the track for success is too important to wing it.* See **Appendices 3A & 3B Worksheets** to get your thoughts organized.

☐ 3. Remember to use your butter voice. Focus on the primary goal—helping your Volunteer to be successful.

☐ 4. Make the commitment to handle negative behavior earlier rather than later. You owe it to your Volunteers to help them *get back on track* and be successful as soon as possible.

☐ 5. Go to www.JuneKenny.com for free training Worksheets, helpful tips on working with Volunteers, and to participate in discussions and to share your ideas.

> *"Before you speak, THINK:*
> T - *Is it TRUE?*
> H - *Is it HELPFUL?*
> I - *Is it INSPIRING?*
> N - *Is it NECESSARY?*
> K - *Is it KIND?"*
>
> *– Anonymous*

☑ Actions I Plan to Take for Compassionate Criticism:

1._____

2._____

3._____

4._____

5._____

6._____

7._____

8._____

APPENDIX 3A: *The ANYBODY Model* WORKSHEET

COMPASSIONATE CRITICISM given with <u>A HEART</u>!
The Anybody Model (♥ ♥ ♥ Motivators)

Useful for anyone including Friends, Acquaintances, Colleagues, or even people with whom there is no significant relationship in place.

A 1. (♥) Opener: **ASK for help**. "I have *a problem* I could use your help with." Or: _____

_____

H 2. "When…" _____
(Describe the specific, ineffective behavior that is **HAPPENING now**)
Active Voice: "When you do XYZ" Passive Voice: "When XYZ occurs"

_____

E 3. (♥) "It causes…" **END result** (Explain **Negative Impact** of this behavior to ministry, your organization, goals or success - *a problem*)

_____

A 4. "I'd appreciate it if you could…" (request **ALTERNATIVE behavior** that fixes *the problem*)

_____

R 5. Together **RESOLVE** *this problem* by engaging in a two-way dialogue – pick best fix

_____

_____

T 6. (♥) Sincere **THANKS** or Appreciation for (*future/hoped for*) cooperation

_____

77

APPENDIX 3B: *Compassionate Criticism – FOR FRIENDS ONLY Model WORKSHEET*

COMPASSIONATE CRITICISM given with A HEART!
(with feelings)
For Friends Only Model (♥♥♥♥Motivators)

This is only successful when used with people who care enough about you to be influenced by your feelings.

(Please note: this is a surprisingly small number of people.)

A 1. (♥) Opener: **ASK for help**. "I have *a problem* I could use your help with." Or: _____

+ *feelings* 2. (♥) "I feel…" ("frustrated", "confused", "disappointed", etc. NOT: "furious", "dumbfounded", "crushed", etc. Do not be overly dramatic.)

_____

_____

H 3. "When…" _____
(Describe the specific, ineffective behavior that is **HAPPENING now**)
Active Voice: "When you do XYZ" Passive Voice: "When XYZ occurs"

_____

E 4. (♥) "It causes…" **END result** (Explain **Negative Impact** of this behavior to ministry, your organization, goals or success - *a problem*)

_____

A 5. "I'd appreciate it if you could…" (request **ALTERNATIVE behavior** that fixes *the problem*)

_____

R 6. Together **RESOLVE** *this problem* by engaging in a two-way dialogue – pick best fix

_____

_____

T 7. (♥) Sincere **THANKS** or Appreciation for *(future/hoped for)* cooperation

#4: Make Your Expectations Clear to Get the Results You Want

So, how do we do that?

Communication is the #1 tool of leadership. It is how we convey the mission, goals and passion of ministry. On a day-to-day basis, communication is how we explain what needs to be done and encourage others to help us do it.

Over the last 20 years of asking corporations about the problems they deal with most, poor communication was consistently cited as the #1 headache. With all the mega-advancements in communication, tele-communication, cell phones, Facebook, Twitter, YouTube, Skype, et.al., how can this be true? Surely we must be communicating better. Or are we just mis-communicating at a faster rate? I am sure we all have anecdotal evidence to suggest the latter.

Churches are not immune. In fact, a pastor once lamented to me that his biggest challenge was not telling others about Christ. "They already know about him. The problem is that what they know about Jesus is not the truth." The task of undoing miscommunication is much harder than making sure the right message is delivered in the first place.

So what are some ways that can help us do that?

This chapter will help you understand how miscommunication happens in the first place, and what you can do to assure that your messages arrive intact.

FOUR PURPOSES OF COMMUNICATION[23]

Did you realize that every time we speak, we expect something from the person with whom we are talking? In fact, just recognizing that those expectations exist is a major step toward improving our communication effectiveness. If we are clear about what we expect to accomplish with this communication, we are in a much better position to make it clear to someone else. All communication can be divided into four purposes, each with a set of expectations on the part of the sender and listener. Miscommunication is an unavoidable outcome when the sender and listener are operating at cross-purposes—even though each may sincerely want to connect with the other.

Let's take a quick look at each purpose and see what is expected of us.

The Four Purposes of Communication

The four purposes are depicted as a pyramid for a reason. The lower levels support the higher levels. We find that without a solid foundation, the higher levels simply do not work effectively.

---

[23]Dr. Lyman Stile and Dr. Richard K. Bommelje, *Listening Leaders: The 10 Golden Rules to Listen, Lead & Succeed*, (Edina, MN: Beavers Pond Press, 2004), 141-166.

SECRET #4: *Make Your Expectations Clear to Get the Results You Want*

LEVEL ONE: SMALL TALK/CHIT CHAT

The first and least risky way to interact with another is at the lowest level – **Small Talk/Chit Chat**. It is important to relationship building both in the workplace and in ministry. Our willingness to spend time at this level will reap big rewards at the higher levels. "How are you today?" "How was your weekend?" "Do you like the *favorite sports* team's chances in the playoffs?" "What's this crazy weather we're having?" "How was your son's baseball tournament last weekend?"

You may ask yourself, "Why would anyone want to have that kind of conversation when there are really important things to discuss and decisions to be made?" If so, let me encourage you to reconsider your position. Making a personal (i.e., not strictly task-focused) connection is one of the foundations of relationship building. It is how we acknowledge the existence of another human being—the bare minimum to start to build a connection.

Listener Expectations at Level One: Small Talk/Chit Chat

1) **Time** – Fortunately not a lot of time, but ZERO is NEVER an effective amount.

2) **Acknowledgment** – If someone says "Hi," it is not a good idea to walk past them in silence. The "you don't exist in my world" approach seldom works well in the long run for building strong working relationships.

3) **Reciprocation** – "How are you?" requires a response. The correct response is "Fine" even if you are not "fine." In addition, a reciprocating question is expected, such as "And how are you?" Please note: In the American culture, typically "How are you?" is not meant as a real question. Its primary purpose is to make human connection—not a request for a medical update.

LEVEL TWO: FEELINGS/EMOTION

At Level Two the message is delivered with an emotional wrapping: frustration, excitement, happiness, confusion, anger, etc., (a.k.a., venting). I know there are folks who would like to skip this phase entirely. Unfortunately, since we are leaders of human beings, emotion comes with the territory. People are trying to figure out if they can trust us with what is in their heart as well as their mind. It is at this level where relationships can deepen and people become allies, supporters, or friends as they learn they can trust us with more than the time of day and the weather report.

> *"People are trying to figure out if they can trust us with what is in their heart as well as their mind."*

Listener Expectations at Level Two: Feelings/Emotion

1) Time. Some, but not unlimited time. No one is expecting you to hang out a shingle and offer on-going psychiatric care. Here is a **TIP TO MANAGE YOUR TIME INVESTMENT:** Decide in advance how much time you can give and then stick to it. Prepare, in advance, an **EXIT STATEMENT** that is both gracious and respectful. Only you can decide how much time you are willing or can give to this kind of verbal support. Having a preplanned exit statement can help you from feeling stuck. For example: "That sounds like an exciting vacation. I'd love to hear more sometime, but I have to run." Or "How frustrating that must be. I hope things work out for you. Good luck." Followed with, "I apologize for rushing off but I am…" ("under a bit of a time crunch right now", "late for a meeting", "need to get back to work", etc.).

2) Show Concern and Empathy (not Sympathy) – i.e., The Gift of Listening. There are two common and all too frequent errors that occur in response to emotional communications. The first major error is more commonly committed by men and the other by women. When someone is venting in frustration, it is usually connected to some kind of problem. No surprise here. Men (and sometimes women) who happen to be fixers by nature listen for 30 seconds, then jump in and tell the sender exactly what he needs to do to solve his problem and get on with life. Male participants in training classes frequently ask, "So, what's wrong with that?" The error is that the sender was not asking for your solution. Their desire was for **the gift of listening**. The real message you have sent is "You are stupid. I, on the other hand, am brilliant—as evidenced by the fact that I can listen for a mere 30 seconds and immediately solve your problem. A little appreciation for my greatness would be nice. Thank you very much."

3) Reciprocation is not expected here! More importantly, it is not wanted. The second major error occurs when women (and some men) are too eager to interrupt with their own similar horrible experience. Imagine a frazzled woman telling you about her hectic morning. She opens with "You won't believe my kids this morning! I couldn't get them out of the house to save my soul! They started arguing and fighting at the breakfast table and...." What do women tend to quickly interject? *"Your kids? Pffft. You should see my kids! They're the worst in the mornings! Let me tell you...."* Oops! Wait a second, wasn't this her story? She wanted our **concern and empathy**, not our competing tale of woe.

Your excellent listening is especially important at **Level Two: Feelings/Emotion** because it is often possible to help someone quickly get through this venting phase and move on to problem-solving. Giving them the **gift of listening** and letting them vent (for a short period of time) could help them calm down enough to move forward and begin to problem-solve. But ignoring the emotions and jumping directly into your solution or your story usually does not work. It can even make things worse.

LEVEL THREE: INFORMATION SHARING

Everyone is familiar with the third purpose – **Information Sharing**. This is where we would all like to be when we are trying to get stuff done—explaining a task, asking for information, discussing ideas, brainstorming solutions, i.e., the nitty-gritty of the day-to-day workplace or church.

What are the expectations for the good listener at **Level Three: Information Sharing**? We are expected to be asking the right questions (at least to ourselves) as we listen to them. "Do I understand what is being said?" "Is this accurate or truthful from my experience?" "Is the message complete or am I missing some parts? Which parts?" And, most importantly, "What do they want me to do with this information?" These questions help us understand their message accurately and know how to take action.

> *"What do they want me to do with this information?"*

When we cannot answer those questions in our own minds, we have an obligation to interact with the sender to clarify whatever we need to know. In other words, it is expected that we will be an active participant in getting the message.

Communication comes from the root word "communes" which means "connection." That is exactly what we are trying to do when we communicate—connect with another person. It cannot be done in a vacuum. It takes mutual effort. And sometimes a lot of effort! The *usual* definition of good communication is getting other people to listen to us, understand us, respond to what we say, and do what we want. The *real* definition, however, is "mutual understanding"—and that takes two. According to George Bernard Shaw, "The problem with communication is the illusion that it has

SECRET #4: *Make Your Expectations Clear to Get the Results You Want*

taken place."[24] Amen to that!

LEVEL FOUR: PERSUASION

Persuasion is the most challenging purpose because it often masquerades as simple **Information Sharing**. What do we need to do when we suspect that the message may be more than just information sharing? Your questioning skills come into play again. Ask the same basic questions you use with **Information Sharing** plus three more.

1) "Is there some personal gain involved if he successfully convinces me to do XYZ?"

2) "Are there other (i.e., opposite) ways to look at this? What are they?"

3) "What is <u>not being said</u> that I should know before agreeing to take action?"

Let me emphasize **Persuasion** is not sinister; we just need to be thoughtful about it. In fact, persuasion is terrific. It is one of a leader's basic skills. We have an idea and we would like help implementing it. So, we need to get buy-in, commitment and enthusiasm that will translate into effort. That is how stuff gets done.

Persuasion does not have to mean manipulation. All of us use our persuasion skills daily. We want other people to believe as we do, support what we support, and help us when help is needed. In truth, pastors must be expert persuaders to be effective. They know how important it is that the truth about Christ reaches those who currently believe the rampant misinformation.

Sharpening your listening skills by figuring out the speaker's purpose is important to you for several reasons. If others are to help you (especially for free), they will be more inclined to do so if they feel you respect them enough to listen. And when you are the

---

[24] George Bernard Shaw (1856-1950), Irish playwright and critic; Nobel Prize in Literature (1925); Academy award/Screenplay for *Pygmalion* (1938).

sender of the message, you can make sure you include the answers to the questions they might (or might not, but should) be asking in their heads: "Why do I need to know this?" and "What do you want me to do with it?" Miscommunication happens when we are not fully aware of where the sender is coming from. Which of the four purposes is in play? Once we sharpen our listening and can successfully identify the four purposes, we have the opportunity to effectively connect.

Communication is definitely a two-way street—with plenty of potholes to fall into along the way. Asking ourselves the right questions as we are listening, and then interacting with the sender to confirm that we got it right, can go a long way toward mutual understanding. Even when we are operating at the same level, however, connection is not guaranteed. Erma Bombeck hit the nail on the head. She said, "It seems rather incongruous that in a society of super-sophisticated communications, we often suffer from a shortage of listeners."[25] You have a wonderful opportunity to excel in a very important area.

TWO SIMPLE RULES TO INCREASE YOUR SUCCESS RATE

I am often asked, "What is the most important thing one can do to become a better communicator?" The answer is simple:

1) **Take 75% Responsibility.** Commit to taking 75% of the responsibility to make sure the correct message is received—whether you are on the sending side or the receiving side. This means **Asking Questions** to understand better and **Paraphrasing** what you thought you heard—just to make sure you got it right.

---

[25] Erma Bombeck (1927-1996), American humorist, syndicated columnist, writer. Known for *The Grass is Always Greener over the Septic Tank and If Life is Just a Bowl of Cherries, What Am I Doing in the Pits?*, and others.

2) **Give Up Multi-Tasking**[26]—**at least when Communicating.** Even if you think you can take care of other business while someone is talking to you, you will not get credit for it in their eyes. As far as they are concerned, you are not listening. In fact, Dr. Clifford Nass in Stanford University research studies has shown that multitasking is not very effective…anywhere. Researchers were trying to uncover the specific skills of great multi-taskers so that the rest of us (less-gifted people) could learn from them. What they discovered surprised even the researchers. The performance of multi-taskers was terrible—contrary to their personal opinions about their own efficiency. Bottom line? Put aside the email, texting, social networking and paperwork and be *in the moment*. Focus on the real, live person in front of your face who is trying to connect with you.

If these two rules are regularly practiced, you will be a better communicator and others will see you that way, too.

MAKING EXPECTATIONS CLEAR

As a Ministry Leader, you probably give people directions all the time. Have you ever given someone directions, were convinced they understood you, and then were surprised by their finished project? You thought everything was clear. They said everything was clear. What on earth happened? How can two smart, well-meaning people agree and still not be thinking the same thing? We may not understand all the reasons for how but we know it happens.

Here is a simple model to assure that your Volunteer really

---

[26] Eyal Ophir, Clifford Nass, and Anthony D. Wagner, "Cognitive control in media multi-taskers," 2009/08/21.

understands what you have asked them to do.

>Step One: State Why the Task is Important
>Step Two: Make the Factual Message Positive
>Step Three: Make the Factual Message Specific
>Step Four: Encourage a 2-way Dialogue

THE HOW TO'S

All four steps are simple and straight-forward. First, make sure both of you are at **Level Three: Information Sharing** before you begin. See, your sharper observation skills are at work already.

> *"If you want to build a ship,*
> *don't drum up people together to collect wood*
> *and don't assign them tasks and work, but rather teach them*
> *to long for the endless immensity of the sea."*
> *— Antoine de Saint-Exupery*[27]

Step One: State Why the Task is Important. *"In order to...."* Where does this task fit in the big-picture? How does it specifically contribute to the success of ministry goals? How does it serve kingdom goals? In other words, why does this need to be done in the first place? Simple? Yes. Easy? Not necessarily. So many tasks associated with ministry are mundane—put up tables and chairs, clean bathrooms, change diapers, make Kool-Aid, sweep floors, pull weeds, pick up trash. No one is denying they all need to be done. But face it—mundane feels unimportant, especially the 100th time you've done it. I have not heard any of these specific skills being hailed as spiritual gifts, have you? The challenge is to help Volunteers grasp how significant their work is to God's great plan—with special attention given to the mundane stuff.

---

[27] Antoine de Saint-Exupery (1900-1944), French aristocrat, writer, poet, pioneering aviator; famous for his novella, *The Little Prince*.

SECRET #4: *Make Your Expectations Clear to Get the Results You Want*

For example, do the nursery workers know that failing to make sure a baby has clean diapers at departure can potentially impact whether mom and dad will trust their little one to their care again? What if these parents are newcomers to church that morning? Will they return? What if they are Volunteers working in another ministry area? Will they feel they can continue serving? A small mundane act can have a vast ripple effect on the spiritual growth of the parents, possibly even on the home environment the child grows up in.

What about the significance of a clean and sparkling restroom? Of course the health department would prefer that your church not spread disease, but how is this possibly going to impact ministry? In many churches, especially larger ones, it is the ladies room where women are inclined to engage in level-one conversations—the first human-touch exchange. "Oh, are you new here?" Or "I don't think we've met before?" Maybe standing side-by-side in close proximity in front of a mirror, staring into someone's face encourages us to say "Hi." Whatever the reason, people meet and greet there. The larger the congregation, the more difficult it is for the newcomer to get noticed. Maybe it is simply the smaller room that is the trigger. The bottom line: if the smaller room is not clean, attractive and fresh smelling, even that small connection will not take place. Don't forget, women are still half the population so it is worth thinking about.

Step Two: Make the Factual Message Positive. *"We (You) need to...do ABC."* Tell the person what you want them to do instead of what not to do. A positive factual message might be stated in this way: "It's important that you are here at the beginning of the team meeting so that we can get started on time." Instead of this negative approach, "Please work on not being late to team meetings."

Here is a surprising fact you may not have considered: Did you know that listening is visual? At least it is for 5 standard deviations of the normal population. We create pictures in our brain of what we are being told. Unfortunately, we do not have a good picture for the word "not." "Do not eat that cheesecake in the freezer!" may be meant to motivate someone (like me, for instance) to make better eating choices. However, what is the picture in my head? Cheesecake, of course, because there is no picture for *not cheesecake*. Cheesecake is now a visual picture on my radar screen

---

We create pictures in our brain of what we are being told. Unfortunately, we do not have a good picture for the word "not."

---

and there is a high likelihood I am moving towards it—not away from it. How effective was the message? Not terribly if my goal was to encourage me to avoid cheesecake. I might have had more success if I had stated the desired behavior. "When I crave something sweet, I'll grab an energy bar." Now my picture is an energy bar. It is a small point to make, I know, but it is critical to shaping the message so that it will be perceived and acted on the way you hope.

Step Three: Make the Factual Message Specific. *"By that I mean...."* Provide the details that describe the behavior you want. If you are asking everyone to be "on time" so that the meeting can start promptly, define what you mean by "on time." One could say the exact time, 9:30 a.m., but that may not be enough for complete clarity. Does your congregation operate on *church time* where everyone knows that meetings always start ten minutes later than posted? Some people feel they are on time if they are pulling into

SECRET #4: *Make Your Expectations Clear to Get the Results You Want*

the parking lot at 9:30 a.m. Consider saying, "Please get here at least five minutes before our meeting to grab your coffee so we can start promptly at 9:30. I want to be respectful of your time." If you are asking someone to clean the bathroom, how do you define clean? If you are asking someone to give a friendly greeting to people who are coming to church, what specifically does that entail? What do you want them to say? What answers do you want them to give to newcomers who may ask predictable questions? Help people get a clearer picture of what is in your head. The specifics help.

Step Four: Encourage a 2-way dialogue. *"What else...?"* The goal is to get the listener to talk about what they thought you said. You had a clear picture in your head. You thought you painted it well. Would you like to know what picture is in their head? You

need to know if they understood, right? The correct question you need to ask may surprise you. **Unfortunately, the most asked question (*"Do you understand?"*) is the one question you should NEVER USE!** (Oops! Did I just violate my own rule— Step Two: Make it Positive? Yes, I did, but please hang in there with me. Specific positive *to do's* are coming, I promise.)

"What's wrong with that?" you ask. "It's what I need to know." There are a number of problems with this frequently asked question. First, you will not get an answer that tells you much. More than likely they are going to say "yes." You have just verbally painted a picture for them. They heard something and painted something themselves. "Do you understand?" is the same

91

as asking, "I have a picture in my head; do you have a picture in yours?" Their predictable "yes" will not tell you if their picture is the same as yours or not. In fact, even when they do not understand what you said, they are probably going to say "yes" anyway. They do not want to look stupid. So, the question gets you nowhere.

Here comes the *make it positive* part. The question that will work is an open-ended question—one that cannot be answered by "yes" or "no" and will get them talking. Closed questions stop dialogue. Open questions promote dialogue which, in this case, is exactly what you need. They usually begin with "What?" or "How?". For example: "What's your understanding of what needs to be done?" (…then they talk. You listen.) "How do you plan to begin this task?" (…then they talk. You listen.)

A gracious way for you to encourage them to talk is to take the responsibility for any possible miscommunications without blaming them. For example: "You know, I don't feel that I was as clear as I meant to be. What's your understanding of this task—just in case I missed something?" By the way, you can say this with 100% honesty 100% of the time. We are NEVER as clear as we meant to be. When you are on the receiving end, use "I know this is important to you so I want to make sure I get it right. This is my understanding of what you need me to do." Tell them your perception of the task and then confirm, "Is that right? Did I miss anything?"

Once you have had a 2-way discussion and are reasonably sure you are both on the same page, ask, "What else could we do to achieve our goal of…(see Step One)?" Asking for a Volunteer's input to support the success of the big-picture goal sends an important message about their value to your ministry. The key to success is to help them tell you about their picture (paraphrasing not parroting) before they set out to achieve the task. Potential miscommunication can be cleared up before it ever turns into a mistake.

SECRET #4: *Make Your Expectations Clear to Get the Results You Want*

> *Sample Dialogue – Meeting Attendance:*
> "In order to start our meetings on time and to successfully complete everything on our agenda, we need to have everyone here and ready to go by 8:30. This means, please get here at least ten minutes before our meeting to grab your coffee or snack so we can start promptly at 8:30. What else can you think of that would help ensure our meetings are efficient and more productive?"

> *Sample Dialogue – Bathroom Maintenance:*
> "The only person-to-person contact someone may have on their first visit to our church might be in the ladies' restroom. That is why it is so important that we have a clean, pleasant and attractive environment to welcome them. That means all of the supplies should be checked before each service, counters and mirrors refreshed, stalls checked for problems, etc. What else could we do to make this a pleasant experience for them?"

Some churches have taken this opportunity to the next level by staffing the ladies' rooms with Volunteer attendants that greet visitors and offer hand lotion, etc. When you ask a seriously-committed Volunteer what else could be done, you may just get an answer.

Use **APPENDIX 4A:** *4-Step Model for Communicating Expectations* to help you think through your next task-related discussion with your Volunteer. When you do your homework up-front to become a more effective communicator, you will be pleasantly surprised by how much more talented and valuable your Volunteers seem.

8½ SECRETS

☑ Action Steps to Get Better Results:

☐ **1. Practice Identifying the Speaker's Purpose/Level.** Respond as a good listener would by fulfilling the expectations the speaker has for you. Observe the positive results you will get.

The Four Purposes of Communication

☐ **2. Take 75% of the Responsibility** for the Communication whether you are speaking or listening. **Ask Questions** to clarify; **Paraphrase** to confirm your understanding.

☐ **3. Stop Multitasking** when communicating. Be *in the moment* and focus on the person in front of you.

☐ **4. Practice the 4-Step Model** for communicating effectively and clearly when explaining your expectations to a Volunteer. Use **APPENDIX 4A:** *4-Step Model for Communicating Expectations* to get your thoughts together.

☐ **5.** Go to www.JuneKenny.com for free training Worksheets, helpful tips on working with Volunteers, to participate in discussions and to share your ideas.

SECRET #4: *Make Your Expectations Clear to Get the Results You Want*

☑ Actions I Plan to Take to Get Better Results:

1. _____

2. _____

3. _____

4. _____

5. _____

6. _____

7. _____

8. _____

"I know you believe you understand what you think I said, but I'm not sure you realize that what you heard is not what I meant."[28]

---

[28] First attributed in print to Robert McCloskey, U.S. State Department, by Marvin Kalb, CBS reporter in *TV Guide*, March 1984. Earlier attribution to "a high government official", Annual Report, Federation of Tax Administrators, 1967. God bless whoever had the insight to utter this clever statement. It nicely sums up the condition of human communication. We need help.

APPENDIX 4A: *4-STEP MODEL for Communicating Expectations* WORKSHEET

Worksheet: 4-Step Model for Communicating Expectations

Communicating Your *Information Sharing Messages* Effectively

Communicate what you expect of others, using clear, specific language. It is one of the best ways to avoid misunderstandings and get the response you want.

1. In order to... _____

_____

_____

(Big Picture Goal/Reasons for/Purpose of/Benefits of doing/Impact to Ministry)

2. We (you) need to... _____

_____

_____

(Stated Positively – What To Do vs. What Not To Do)

3. This means... _____

_____

_____

("By that I mean"... The Specifics)

4. What else...? _____

_____

_____

(Open-ended Question to explore **Understanding** & **Other Ideas** to achieve **Big Picture Goal**)

#5: Run Meetings that Don't Drive Volunteers Crazy (or Away!)

So, how do we do that?

Do you have regular meetings with your Volunteer staff? Are the meetings really necessary? Do your meetings start and end on time? Do you accomplish your goals? Do your Volunteers know you even have goals? You might not realize it but your answers to these questions may be driving away your most talented Volunteers.

Highly skilled and willing Volunteers are often the busiest people you will meet. Everyone wants a piece of their time and talent. Why? They get things done. Like most Volunteers, they want to be successful and make a difference. They want to know that their time has been well-invested.

Poorly planned or poorly run meetings are reasons why Volunteers decline to renew a commitment to serve especially when the tradeoff is lost family time. Unfortunately, when a wasteful reputation is established, only the newbies in the congregation will venture into your quagmire. You may still get Volunteers for clearly defined projects or events, but finding people who will commit to on-going ministry support becomes more and more difficult.

It is all too easy for a Ministry Leader to adopt the rationale "You just can't get good help these days." Perhaps, however, the truth is you are driving your Volunteers crazy! They may want to serve. They may even want to serve with you! But they don't want their time needlessly squandered.

How can you do a better job of honoring their time and energy? The answer is simple: plan and run more efficient and more effective meetings that set and accomplish bigger (not smaller) goals for the Kingdom.

It may sound surprising to you, but if you want more commitment from Volunteers, make the job more important not less important. "But I can't even get them to show up (or call to cancel) now! How can I get them to do even more?" Have you ever considered that what you are asking of them may be perceived as meaningless, redundant or not worth doing? If it doesn't get done, "So what?" they think. Miss a meeting? "No big deal." Make it worth their time and effort.

So, how do you make your meetings worth the effort? Make every meeting a great one! There are EIGHT CHARACTERISTICS of great meetings. Do your meetings have all of them? Which one(s) do you need to add or strengthen?

EIGHT CHARACTERISTICS OF GREAT MEETINGS

CHARACTERISTIC 1:
 A Clear Reason to Meet (The ABC's of Meetings)
CHARACTERISTIC 2:
 A Realistic Time Allotment that is Honored
CHARACTERISTIC 3:
 All the Right People are Represented at the Meeting
CHARACTERISTIC 4:
 Advance Notice of When, Where and What
CHARACTERISTIC 5:
 A Visible, Well-Prepared and Timed Agenda
CHARACTERISTIC 6:
 An Effective Leader/Facilitator who Manages the Time Topics, and Conversation
CHARACTERISTIC 7:
 A Brief but Essential Meeting Recap to Summarize Key Actions or Decisions

CHARACTERISTIC 8:

Periodic Evaluations of Meeting Effectiveness (for truly great meetings)

Let's take a quick look at what is really involved in producing a great meeting. Fortunately for all of us, it is not brain surgery. We can do this.

CHARACTERISTIC 1: **A Clear Reason to Meet (The ABC's of Meetings)**

Have a clear purpose for every meeting. Always ask; "Why is this meeting necessary? What do we want to accomplish by meeting together? Can we accomplish our goal another way?" Meeting without a clear goal is like going on a trip without a destination and without a map. The point is: a meeting may, or may not, be the best way to achieve the goal. **START WITH THE ASSUMPTION** that it is not the best choice. Then, if you cannot think of any other way to get the job done, have a meeting.

Don't get me wrong, there are legitimate reasons that justify meeting together: pot-luck dinners, event-planning sessions, annual congregation meetings to name a few. To help you sort out the kinds of meetings worth having, check out the *ABC's* of Meetings. They are: (A) Association, (B) Brainstorming, (C) Consensus, and (D) "Data Dumping" (known in more polite circles as "Data Dissemination").

A-Meetings: Association Meetings have the primary purpose of community building, strengthening relationships, celebrating together, worshiping and my favorite pastime—eating. The church dinner (a.k.a., "breaking bread") is an important element in building strong church interpersonal relationships and genuine love for one another. In fact, it is enough of a reason to meet all by itself. Is it possible we ought to be having more of those **A-meetings**? Okay, I know. Who has that kind of time? Nevertheless,

Hebrews 10:25 (NIV) suggests it is a high priority: *"Let us not give up meeting together.* Some are in the habit of doing this. Instead, let us cheer each other up with words of hope. *Let us do it all the more* as you see the day coming when Christ will return." (*emphasis mine*)

With a little planning, some of the elements and benefits of **A-Meetings** can be regularly and easily worked into B, C or D-meetings. If relationship building is one of your on-going team goals, try including a few **A-Meeting** components into your other meetings. For example, if you did not want to take time from the meeting but still want to foster some connectivity, plan for coffee and snacks to be available 15-minutes before the meeting. Publicize it. Encourage participants to come a little early.

B-Meetings: Brainstorming meetings have the primary purpose of providing a focused opportunity for creative thinking, strategic thinking and Volunteer input. The **B-Meeting** makes a powerful Volunteer appreciation statement. You are showing that you value Volunteers' experience, expertise and talent by creating a forum that encourages their intellectual input and deeper involvement. It is a way of saying that they have legitimately become your partners in ministry.

Good **B-Meetings** typically end with a list of creative options rather than one final decision. These cream-of-the-crop ideas are then analyzed for cost, labor, time and how effectively they will achieve the ultimate goal. This analysis generally takes more than the nano-second it has been known to get. If done well, the analysis becomes the critical factor in making the best decisions—yielding the best results. The biggest downfall of most **B-Meetings** is that too often we short-circuit the "B" process. We too quickly criticize an idea as impractical or unworkable. So what if it is? That so-called crazy idea may be the stimulus that generates the great idea you can use. Jumping in too early is equivalent to throwing a bucket of cold water on the enthusiasm and creativity of the entire group. To get some great ideas for running an effective brainstorming session see *"Rules for Brainstorming"* **in APPENDIX 5A**.

C-Meetings: Consensus Meetings have the primary purpose of nailing down the final decision. We have agreed upon a clear plan of action. It's GO TIME! Let's implement!

One of the biggest frustrations for the high-energy, task-driven Volunteer is coming to a **B-Meeting** thinking it is a **C-Meeting**. Maybe it was never your plan to nail down a final decision. Your intention was to expand options and flesh out ideas. Your Volunteer, however, was understandably frustrated when, at the end of the 2-hour meeting, the expected decision failed to appear. The problem was lack of clarity. Had the Volunteer known your purpose, he probably would have felt the time well-spent instead of thinking you were disorganized, indecisive and wasted his time.

D-Meetings: Data Dumping Meetings have the primary purpose of making sure that all key players have the information they need. Everyone is on the same page at the same time. If you anticipate confusion, a need for a clarifying discussion or want to short-circuit the rumor-mill by releasing the information all at once, a D-Meeting may be your best option. In all other cases there might be more creative alternatives that work as well: conference call, email, snail mail, texting, phone tree, traveling document, web-posting (public or private), Facebook Groups, Twitter, etc.

Of course, meeting types can often be successfully combined. The key is clarity—most importantly, yours, then theirs. Why are we meeting? Are we trying to build community or relationships? Do we need input for creative alternatives to what we have been doing or great ideas to do them better? Are we ready to finalize our plan and start the implementation phase? Do we have a ton of information but no assurance that anybody will actually read an email? If relationship-building is one of your on-going team goals, regularly include an **A-Meeting** activity into or before the meeting.

THE THREE BIGGEST AREAS OF FRUSTRATION FOR VOLUNTEERS

- Meetings that do not start and stop on time: this is an easy fix if you are committed. Remember Nike's slogan: "Just Do It!"

- The over-used, mind-numbing **D-Meeting:** use creative alternatives to transmit that data, please.

- The **B-Meeting** and **C-Meeting** mix-up: I think I hear a little voice saying, "No problem there. We'll just combine B & C into one meeting. How efficient are we?!" That might have merit if efficiency equaled effectiveness, but it does not. Rushing to judgment and jumping into implementation short-circuits the process of making good results-focused decisions. Speed is not necessarily the best way to produce the best results. Yes, we may have gotten some positive results, but were they the best we could have done with what God gave us to work with?

Does this scenario sound familiar? A team is meeting to discuss the need to "do something to appreciate our Volunteers." Within 30 seconds, someone says "Let's have a Volunteer Appreciation Dinner." The team is now off to the races planning a dinner. No one has stopped to ask "Is a dinner the best thing we could do to show our Volunteers how much they mean to us?"

What are our other options? In reality there might be dozens if we take the time to look for them. What are the three best ideas? Now let's analyze each to see how it achieves the desired results. How much money do we need for the number of Volunteers we have? How many labor-hours are needed to implement each choice? What is the anticipated impact? Who might fall through the cracks? What are we going to do for them, if anything? Which idea will touch the most Volunteers?

The research teams can report back at the next meeting (a true **"C-Meeting"**) where we will finalize our best option based on their data and input. Then, we jump full-force into planning...our BEST OPTION. A dinner may turn out to be the best choice, but it also may not. We owe it to good stewardship to do our due diligence.

CHARACTERISTIC 2: **A Realistic Time Allotment that is Honored**

Start and stop on time and quit trying to stuff 10 pounds of potatoes into an 8-pound sack. The key to success is preparation. List all agenda items you would like to consider for this meeting. Ask yourself: "Realistically, how much time will telling, discussing or deciding take?" Do this with each proposed topic. Now comes the hard part. If you are like me, you now have planned a meeting that will last until midnight! Decide which are the most important items. Put those into the agenda. Can any of the remaining topics be communicated in any other way? If not, their importance may rate them a spot at the next meeting. Be ruthless—in a Christian way, of course.

At the meeting, post the agenda with the time allotments clearly in view. Ask for your team's help in sticking to the agenda in order to efficiently achieve this meeting's goals. Should a discussion start to take on a life of its own, briefly stop the meeting and ask the team what they would like to do. Ask: "Is this something we can complete in the time allotted? If not, should we continue to discuss this right now or put it in the *wigbitty*? **WGBTI** stands for the "We'll Get Back To It" file. It is usually represented by a blank flip chart page visible to all. Items posted here will be considered for the next (or some future) meeting. It is an assurance that someone's idea or concern will not be forgotten. If **WGBTI** is hard for you to say with a straight face, call it a "parking lot" or be creative and come up with your own name. Whatever you call it, it can

103

definitely help you stay on track.

If, however, the team decides to complete this discussion item, the agenda needs to be immediately amended by deleting some other *on deck* topic. You will be amazed at how focused your team can become when they have responsibility for the efficiency and effectiveness of their meeting.

CHARACTERISTIC 3: **All the Right People are Represented at the Meeting**

Be sure to include decision makers, technical or content experts (when needed), those impacted by the decision and those expected to successfully implement the plan. How often have you found that you cannot make a decision because the right person was missing in action or not even invited? Planning and preparation eliminates this mid-meeting crisis.

CHARACTERISTIC 4: **Advance Notice of When, Where and What**

Be sure to include this important data: what to prepare, what to bring, topics to discuss, and who is responsible. See *"Sample Meeting Announcement/Agenda"* in **APPENDIX 5B**.

CHARACTERISTIC 5: **A Visible, Well-Prepared and Timed Agenda**

The announcement/agenda is sent in advance to help participants prepare. In addition, during the meeting post a larger flip chart agenda with time estimates. The key is visible at all times. You want people to be aware of how they are using their time. A visible, timed agenda helps everyone stay focused. A wall clock in the room is also a good investment.

CHARACTERISTIC 6: **An Effective Leader who Manages the Time, Topics and Conversation**

- **Manage the Time:** This is not your job alone. Your team becomes co-responsible for this goal when you use a posted, timed agenda and a **WGBTI** option for tabled items. If you find it difficult to facilitate a discussion and watch the clock at the same time, ask a team member to be the meeting timer. She will notify you when you have "X" number of minutes remaining on a topic. Then you simply ask the team what they want to do to proceed. Remember, if they choose to continue the current discussion, an *on-deck* topic needs to be deleted to compensate.

- **Manage the Topics:** You have planned the agenda. The topics are yours. You have guesstimated how much time is appropriate for each. Your accuracy determines your success. Practice makes perfect.

  Other things that help manage the topic: Do the attendees need handouts or visual aids to make the discussion run smoothly? Prepare them in advance. Better yet, send the participants the important information to review and consider prior to the meeting. When it comes to decision-making, many people prefer the chance to sleep on it before being asked to make a decision. Help them to help you by being prepared to participate in a smoothly run, effective meeting that accomplishes its goals.

- **Manage the Conversation:** This can be a challenge when there are people who talk too much or people who will not talk at all. The goal of a discussion is to uncover the relevant thoughts, ideas and opinions about the topic and enough accurate data to make a reasonably decent decision. This is usually easier said than done.

Implement a Code of Conduct

The #1 guarantee to smooth communication flow is a team **Code of Conduct**. See sample in **APPENDIX 5C**. Meeting **Codes of Conduct** usually include important expectations like: arrive on time, be prepared, have an open mind during discussions, allow others to speak without interruptions, treat each other with respect, etc. They go a long way in reinforcing a cultural norm of respect and love for one another. It is especially powerful when the team has taken the time to generate its own list. Some churches have even adopted a scripturally based **"Behavioral Covenant"** for their entire congregations.[29] This church-wide covenant can be a great start to creating your meeting **Code of Conduct**. See **APPENDIX 5D** for an example.

Provide a Communication Traffic Cop (CTC)

Code of Conduct or not, in the heat of battle, people often forget the basics—even Christians. So, the second thing that will help you manage the conversation is someone in the role of **CTC** (Communication Traffic Cop—uniform optional).

The **CTC's** job is to:
1. give the green light to people who wish to contribute ideas.
2. make sure that each person is allowed to finish his comment before another is allowed to begin talking.
3. politely interrupt the interrupters and remind them that Susan wasn't finished yet.
4. address the inevitable red herring comments unrelated to the topic at hand. "That seems to be taking us a little off point from the topic. Would you

---

[29] Faith Covenant Church *(www.4fcc.org)*, Farmington Hills, Michigan, Evangelical Covenant Denomination.

mind if we put this on the **WGBTI**[30] for now and finish the current discussion?" Or "Could you help us connect your idea to our _____ topic?"

Any team member is free to assume the **CTC** role when someone is preventing others from completing their statements. Managing the communication flow is the joint responsibility of all. Over time it will become second nature and part of your meeting culture.

Provide a Discussion Facilitator

The **CTC** is a role you, as leader, can assume or you may assign it to a **Discussion Facilitator** which frees you to participate more fully in the discussion itself. The discussion facilitator becomes responsible for shepherding the agenda to successful conclusion by managing the communication flow and watching the time.

IDEAS TO HELP THE DISCUSSION FACILITATOR
Is someone hogging the microphone or conversation?

Put a time limit on how long individuals can present their ideas, concerns or opinions during a discussion—two minutes, five minutes, or ? The rule applies to everyone. Use a stopwatch for accuracy and fairness. You can also decide to limit the number of times someone may speak about a single topic. Make sure everyone knows the discussion guidelines in advance—no mid-discussion surprises, please.

---

[30] WGBTI – term used for postponing agenda items, *We'll Get Back To It.*

What can I do about the incessant interrupter?

The **CTC** is your first line of defense but you could also minimize interruptions by introducing a speaking tool (a ball, rod or other squishy projectile) to keep the discussion moving in a positive direction. Purchase a small colorful, foam ball/rod that can be tossed around the table as the discussion progresses. Only the person holding the ball/rod has the floor. In addition, it may be helpful to establish a time limit for each speaker. When finished, he will throw the ball/rod to the next speaker. The team members and the interrupter are much more aware of the rudeness factor when it is obvious that the interrupter does not have the ball/rod. This *half in jest—all in earnest* strategy creates a light-hearted fun environment that deals indirectly with an awkward situation.

What can I do when the discussion goes on and on and on?

Call for a straw vote to check the group's leanings. If the vote is close, you may want to discuss it further. If it is not close, immediately call for a motion to take some specific action. Votes can be public (e.g., show of hands) or private (e.g., slips of paper).

How can I encourage the quieter person to express his or her ideas?

The more-introverted folks prefer considering in advance what they are going to say. You can help them prepare for the discussion by sending out important information prior to the meeting. They will pre-think the topic, formulate their opinions and more comfortably contribute when they do not have to compose on the spot. You can also vary the discussion process by including an opportunity to write questions on 3x5 cards. These are then submitted to the discussion leader who presents them to the group for consideration. And, of course, be diligent about managing the non-stop talker and interrupter more effectively! Quieter individuals rarely interrupt the interrupter to get their point across.

CHARACTERISTIC 7: **A Brief but Essential Meeting Recap to Summarize Key Actions or Decisions**

Be sure to include:
- Who has committed to do what
- Next meeting date and time
- Statement of thanks or appreciation
- Kingdom impact of this ministry or their contributions

"Good meeting tonight! We nailed down the final pieces that need to be completed for next month's ministry fair/recruitment event. Pat, you are going to meet with Luke to arrange for advertisements to be posted on the website and in the bulletin. Sam, you will be lining up the set-up crew, and Pete, you'll recruit the clean-up crew for the event. Aiden and Kaitlyn will split the list of the remaining ministries, extend invitations to participate and follow-up with them. Matt and Paul, you are in charge of soliciting at least twenty more door prizes. We'll plan on meeting again next Tuesday night at 7:00-8:30 pm. This ministry fair is really going to help a lot of our new people get connected in the right places. The ministries will be able to do more and the Volunteers, themselves, are going to be blessed. Thanks again for being a part of this team. See you next week."

CHARACTERISTIC 8: **Periodic Evaluation by the Team (for truly great meetings)**

Do not be fearful of this. The team is really evaluating itself—not you. Business leaders have always known that "What gets measured gets fixed." Churches are run by human beings. You are safe to assume that any human-run organization is in need of fixing. God already knows we are *works in progress* and loves us anyway! We should never be afraid of asking ourselves, "How are we doing?" "What could we be doing better?" To get started, see a ***Sample Meeting Evaluation Form*** in **APPENDIX 5E**.

This meeting is concluded. Thank you all for your focused attention on the essential elements of a successful meeting. Sharpening your meeting skills will go a long way toward keeping talented Volunteers engaged with you in God's work. Please turn to the next page to see who needs to do what by when.

SECRET #5: *Run Meetings that Don't Drive Volunteers Crazy (or Away!)*

☑ Action Steps to Create Great Meetings:

☐ 1. **Try your best NOT to have a meeting!** First, identify your goal. What do you want to accomplish? Can you achieve it any other way? If not, then, and only then, have a meeting. See **APPENDIX 5B:** *Sample Meeting Announcement/Agenda* to help you plan that unavoidable meeting.

☐ 2. Check to see how many of the **8 CHARACTERISTICS** of Successful Meetings you are utilizing right now. Add the missing pieces.

☐ 3. Help your team develop a **Code of Conduct** that shifts the responsibility for a successful meeting to every participant—not just you. This alone will make your life so much easier. See **APPENDICES 5C-D** to get started.

☐ 4. Buy a soft, colorful foam ball or other squishy projectile and a timer. Use them.

☐ 5. Please, please, please start and stop your meetings on time—no matter what.

☐ 6. Go to www.JuneKenny.com for free training Worksheets, helpful tips on working with Volunteers, to participate in discussions and to share your ideas.

"Time is the only capital that any human being has and the thing that he can least afford to waste or lose."
– Thomas Edison

☑ Actions I Plan to Take to Create Great Meetings:

1. _____

2. _____

3. _____

4. _____

5. _____

6. _____

7. _____

8. _____

APPENDIX 5A: *Rules for Brainstorming*

6 RULES FOR BRAINSTORMING

Rule #1: Have fun! Unleash your RIGHT BRAIN. Don't worry, LEFT BRAIN analysis comes later.

Rule #2: The Goal is QUANTITY not QUALITY. even CRAZY IDEAS have value. Ideas breed more ideas. The more the merrier.

Rule #3: Set a time limit for brainstorming to create a sense of urgency and keep the energy level high.

Rule #4: No idea is criticized (*at this time*). You don't want to be the guy who throws the bucket of cold water on the group's enthusiasm and creativity. Instead try combining ideas using them to trigger more ideas.

Rule #5: Break into two or more groups if there are enough people. Friendly competition will raise the bar and add fun! Each group often takes off on a different track preventing GROUP THINK.

Rule #6: Capture all of the ideas on flip chart, post-it notes, etc. for the ANALYSIS SESSION to follow.

ANALYSIS SESSION:

During this session, first **CONNECT** ideas together wherever possible. Second, **RANK** the ideas by categories that are most important to you. For example: COST (LOW - MEDIUM - HIGH), LABOR REQUIRED (L-M-H), POTENTIAL POSITIVE IMPACT (L-M-H), or any other category that helps you make the best decision to get the most bang for the buck (i.e., to be a good steward of the resources God has given you).

APPENDIX 5B: *Sample Meeting Announcement/Agenda*

Your LOGO here

MEETING ANNOUNCEMENT / AGENDA

FOR: *(Your Team Name Here)*

LEADER (s):

PARTICIPANTS:

Date: _____ time: _____ TO _____

MEETING LOCATION _____

WHAT WE WANT TO ACCOMPLISH:

PLEASE BRING OR DO:

PROPOSED AGENDA:

WHO RESP.	EST. TIME	NEXT ACTIONS REQUIRED	BY WHOM	BY WHEN

We commit to supporting each other and Church leadership in implementing and maintaining our Behavioral Covenant.

APPENDIX 5C: *Sample Meeting Code of Conduct*

Our Ground Rules for Effective Meetings

1. All of us will take the responsibility to make every meeting as effective and productive as possible.

2. Our interactions with each other will always be grace-filled and loving.

3. We agree to start and stop our meetings promptly because everyone's time is valuable and we want to respect it. We will make every effort to attend every meeting (barring emergencies), and arrive in time to allow an "on-time" start and stay until the meeting has ended.

4. We agree to participate fully in discussions by:
   - being prepared in advance when appropriate
   - listening carefully and respectfully to others with an open mind
   - staying focused on the topic at hand
   - not interrupting others but allowing them to finish their thought
   - sharing our ideas and concerns
   - always attacking the problem, not the person or their ideas

5. If sensitive matters are shared, we will treat that information with confidentiality by not discussing it outside of the meeting.

6. Other?

7. Other?

> **PLEASE NOTE:**
> A Meeting Code of Conduct, Ground Rules, or Behavioral Covenant is always more successful when the team creates their own. (See sample Behavioral Covenant on next page.)

APPENDIX 5D: *Sample Behavioral Covenant*

Faith Covenant Church[31]
Behavioral Covenant

"The fruit of the Spirit is love, joy, peace, patience, kindness, goodness, faithfulness, gentleness, and self-control...." Galatians 5:22-23 (ESV)

We have been saved by the Grace of our Lord Jesus Christ through faith. We will therefore conduct ourselves in a manner that reflects this Grace as recognized through the fruit of the Holy Spirit.

At Faith Covenant Church we believe we will thrive and grow when we are free to share our views, and we believe that the congregation will receive our views in the spirit of Grace and Love.

We commit to conducting ourselves in a manner that will reflect our Lord's Grace, will create and maintain a culture in which individuals speak their views kindly, gently and with self-control knowing they will be received with goodness, patience and peace by the listeners, even when viewpoints differ.

We commit to supporting each other and church leadership in implementing and maintaining this Behavioral Covenant.

---

[31] Faith Covenant Church *(www.4fcc.org)*, Farmington Hills, Michigan, Evangelical Covenant Denomination.

APPENDIX 5E: *Sample Meeting Evaluation*

Ministry _____

Date _____

HOW ARE WE DOING?

Time is precious. We want to use it to make the greatest impact for God.

1. How do you rate the overall effectiveness of our meetings at this time?

   -10 -9 -8 -7 -6 -5 -4 -3 -2 -1   0   +1 +2 +3 +4 +5 +6 +7 +8 +9 +10

	Never				Always
2. WE HAVE...clarity of meeting purpose	0	1	2	3	4	5
3. WE USE OUR...time efficiently	0	1	2	3	4	5
4. OUR COMMUNICATION is... respectful and grace-filled	0	1	2	3	4	5
5. OUR FOCUS...centers on making the highest positive impact with the resources available	0	1	2	3	4	5
6. WE HAVE...clarity of next steps (who does what by when)	0	1	2	3	4	5

7. What could we do to improve the effectiveness of future meetings?

8. What meeting alternatives could work for us in our situation and still allow us to achieve our goals?

DIRECTIONS: For consistently effective meetings, perform a quarterly, semi-annually, or whenever you notice the energy is starting to drain from your team meetings. Ask a Volunteer to tabulate the results (calculate averages) and distribute to team members. At the next meeting facilitate a solution-finding session based on your collected data. It is the job of the entire team to determine next best steps to become the most effective team possible. **Ownership is the secret ingredient.**

#6: Tap into Built-In Enthusiasm

So, how do we do that?

This chapter will give you some ideas for expanding your Volunteer base by uncovering what motivates those still *sitting on the bench*. Who knows? They might (actually, they do) have talents you never dreamed of that will translate into new and exciting ways to support your ministry goals.

MOTIVATORS

There are tons of motivators that appeal to individual Volunteers—many that you can quickly incorporate into the job design or your leadership style. You already know the most popular ones: food, fun and fame. Churches have honed the food motivation to a fine art and I am glad they have. Breaking bread together solidifies bonds and communicates "we are family." Fun is pretty well developed, too. However, fame defined in its most generic form as "recognition" could probably use some work. Accurately recognizing a Volunteer's positive impact can be hit or miss depending on the church—and the Ministry Leader. A booster shot of **SECRET #2: *Encourage with Credibility*** will help guarantee your recognition will hit the bullseye. Check out **APPENDIX 6A: *Motivation Self-Assessment*** for a more complete list of individual motivators. Directions are included for how to use this as a team-building activity.

DEMOTIVATORS

While motivators are important, they often are not enough to overcome demotivators. There are three serious demotivators I believe you need to eliminate or, at least, minimize. Their power comes from the fact that they are systemic in nature and usually invisible. They impact your entire church culture and therefore touch almost everyone. Kudos to your church if you have managed to avoid these three systemic demotivators:

1. **LACK OF EXPECTATION**
2. **TOO FEW or OBSTRUCTED PATHWAYS**
3. **SELF-LIMITING OPPORTUNITIES**

All of us are called to serve. Ephesians 2:10 says, "For *we are God's handiwork,* created in Christ Jesus *to do good works,* which God prepared in advance for us to do." In addition, 1 Peter 4:10 explains, "God has given each of you a gift from his great variety of spiritual gifts. *Use them well to serve one another.*"[32]

Unfortunately, not everyone seems to know that, do they? It is not that we haven't asked for help enough. There seems to be some kind of appeal almost every Sunday. So, where is the big disconnect? I believe these three demotivators create the perfect storm to dampen participation over and over again in churches.[33] Hopefully you are the exception. If not, what could you do in your unique situation to minimize the negative impact of each of these?

1. LACK OF EXPECTATION

This is an offense that is committed by both pastors and their congregations. Is serving viewed as natural as breathing at your church? Does everyone know that serving is essential to spiritual development? James 2:26 tells us, "As the body without the spirit

---

[32] Ephesians 2:10, NIV; 1 Peter 4:10, NLT (*emphasis mine*)

[33] Christian non-profit organizations have a slightly different challenge. Since they do not typically have ready-made audiences to tap into, their Volunteer solution lies in intentionally and aggressively affiliating with as many existing congregations (big or small) as they can. The goal is to be seen as an extension of each churches' ministries. You become one of the many options for Volunteers to become a blessing to others. However, the same rules apply as spelled out in Secret #7—jobs also need to be designed to attract the widest range of participants.

SECRET #6: *Tap into Built-In Enthusiasm*

is dead, so faith without works is dead also." "And without faith it is impossible to please God." [34]

Or, is it possible that your church leadership has thrown in the towel and assumed they can only count on the regulars? Really? Is 100% participation too big for God's vision? I do not know about you, but I don't want to be the one to tell him that. More people would participate if they knew that serving is as much a blessing to the giver as it is to the receiver. It is one of the biggest secrets on the planet. When we do something for the benefit of another (with a right heart), God gives us a surprise gift in return. I have talked with hundreds of Volunteers who say they are the ones who have been blessed. Maybe your church could benefit from preaching **Expectations** and **Blessings** more frequently. Never be shy about extending this opportunity to anyone. You are giving them a gift! You are giving Volunteers a life-changing opportunity to experience a very special blessing that God has planned for them.

2. TOO FEW or OBSTRUCTED PATHWAYS

Do you have enough Volunteers? How easy is it to begin to serve in your church? Are the pathways to service obvious and open? These may sound like rhetorical questions, but they are not. I have worked with many churches large and small. There is an all too common problem afoot—too few pathways into service or pathways bottlenecked by single decision-makers who are so swamped that decisions often get delayed or forgotten.

Too Few Pathways:

In one larger church (over 1,000 attendees) the main path to service was serving as a Greeter. No matter what skills or talents were being offered, the Volunteer *wannabe* had to be a Greeter for at least six months—or until *the Second Coming*—

---

[34] James 2:26; Hebrews 11:6a, NIV

whichever came first. This is not a joke. Fear of being stuck in a job that doesn't fit is a serious demotivator. Needless to say there was more than one semi-reluctant Greeter on hand each Sunday to welcome the newcomers. Apparently the *de facto* screening process was simply watching him for six months to make sure he…? Did what? What qualities or talents were we looking for? Singers and musicians seemed to be the only ones to successfully avoid this requirement. To their credit, performing arts ministries typically know what they are looking for. Other ministry areas seem to be a little more *loosey-goosey*, which is one of the problems. If you do not know what you are looking for, is it a surprise that you are not finding many?

Bottlenecked Pathways:

I have seen this occur in many churches, as well. Have you? On a somewhat regular basis, someone complains, "We need more Volunteers!" The pastor agrees to do the semi-annual "Servant's Heart" sermon or the more popular "Guilt: the Gift that Keeps on Giving." Appeals are placed in the bulletin. Cards are filled out and placed in collection plates (unless this has happened one too many times before and the congregation has been conditioned not to bother). Why is this? My guess: the office was not prepared to handle the flood of cards that came in. The pile sat. Some cards eventually made it all the way to the next bottleneck—i.e., Ministry Leaders who were swamped or lacked the necessary administrative support. In fact, they were probably too busy trying to do ministry and wishing they had

SECRET #6: *Tap into Built-In Enthusiasm*

a few Volunteers. Do you think they could have benefited from a few short-term Volunteers specifically recruited to help with the sorting?

3. **SELF-LIMITING OPPORTUNITIES**

Are your Volunteer opportunities primarily designed for a narrow group of people? Do you offer the same type of job over and over? Are you creating jobs that fit all eight of the potential Volunteer categories, expanding your appeal to potential workers? This is so important that we will explore this in the next chapter, **SECRET #7: *Restructure Volunteer Opportunities to Expand Your Volunteer Base.***

Almost **UNIVERSAL MOTIVATORS**

Once you have dealt with the above issues, you should be able to honestly say:
- We preach the *Expectation*
- We have lots of **UNOBSTRUCTED PATHWAYS**
- We have all eight job categories aplenty
- We even have **FOOD, FUN AND FAME** going for us
- Our current Volunteers are happy and motivated

Now, what else could you do to draw those into serving who seem to be spectators? Let's talk about some tried and true strategies to get the remaining people *off the bench* and *into the game*. While individuals can be inspired by a wide array of motivators, there are three very powerful motivators that will influence almost all human beings. These give you more bang for the buck, so to speak. The good news is that they are free and easily incorporated into your ministry culture. However, they generally do not happen by accident. What are you currently doing to incorporate these *almost* universal motivators?

Almost UNIVERSAL MOTIVATORS:
VOLUNTEERS WANT:

1. **to know and be known**
2. **to be part of something bigger than themselves**
3. **to make a positive difference – somewhere – for someone**

1. VOLUNTEERS WANT TO KNOW AND BE KNOWN

Volunteers do not want to be nameless faces in the crowd. They want someone to know who they are—even if it is just a small group of people—their team members or Sunday school class. On Sunday, they would like someone to smile and say "Hello" and be glad to see them. This one is a simple fix. Individual Ministry Leaders can invest the extra time to know a little more about their Volunteers and help them get to know each other better. Providing quick team-building activities at regular team meetings will foster relationships and help Volunteers to bond with each other and with you.

Even a passive technique such as using nametags can help. It may be a small detail but I strongly recommend printing (not writing) both the first and last name. Most of the time, nametags usually have first names only. Why is this? Much of the time this is done intentionally to reinforce a casual (read "welcoming") church culture. Using first and last names is often perceived as more formal (read "stiff" and "standoffish"). The problem is that first names do not help new people remember those they have met. Also, it is more difficult to reconnect. Especially in larger churches, there can be dozens with the name of Sam or Luke or Linda. Church directories have not started alphabetizing by first

SECRET #6: *Tap into Built-In Enthusiasm*

name, have they? I rest my case.

What could you do to make it easier for your Volunteers to get to know each other? Brainstorm a list. Start implementing some of those great ideas.

2. **VOLUNTEERS WANT TO BE PART OF SOMETHING BIGGER THAN THEMSELVES**

Volunteers want to belong. This is not a new concept. Just look at the multi-billion dollar sports industry—team loyalty, wearing team gear, team pride, celebrating victories. There is a deep human need being met by identifying with and being accepted by an organization that is bigger and more powerful than oneself. In fact, motivators #1 and #2 are two important reasons why teens also join street gangs. I am not recommending that you rush out and create a secret handshake, but we could all do a better job of letting Volunteers know they are really on our team. That they belong. That we know their names and faces. And that we actually care about them.

They are our partners in ministry. What could you do to make it more obvious that your Volunteers really do belong to God's Army—and your Platoon in particular?

3. **VOLUNTEERS WANT TO MAKE A POSITIVE DIFFERENCE – SOMEWHERE – FOR SOMEONE**

They want their time, effort and talent to be used to achieve something positive. Communication is your #1 tool. Have you taken the time to communicate what a blessing each and every Volunteer is to those they serve? Do you intentionally and regularly share poignant stories of transformed lives or needs met? These positive-impact stories fill Volunteers' love buckets and inspire them to continue. This is the stuff that will warm their hearts and let them know they have truly made a difference. "Good job" or "Atta-boy" is not enough.

The K.I.S.S.

Since positive contribution is such a critical element for satisfaction, it is important that Volunteers have a successful experience—every time. In fact, isn't that one of the essential responsibilities of any effective leader? The leader does what it takes to help each worker achieve maximum success. Obviously, if training is needed, you make that happen. But even if they have all of the skills needed to do the job, success is not guaranteed. There is a way, however, to almost guarantee it. The Apostle Paul had the idea first. "Greet one another with a kiss of love."[35] I think it is safe to say Paul was probably not referring to Volunteers *per se*. It is still a nice idea, don't you think? Each new Volunteer could and should be greeted with a very special kind of K.I.S.S.:

K – As soon as possible, tell them about the **KINGDOM IMPACT** of the ministry they are entering and of the specific tasks they will be performing. It is amazing how easily we lose sight of how our simple tasks are a blessing to others. **KINGDOM IMPACT** is listed first for a reason. It is the most important one! Understanding the difference we can make—the potential positive impact—is one of the biggest motivators for Volunteer engagement and retention. If we drop the ball in any area, let it not be this one.

I – Tell them all of the **INFORMATION** they will need to be successful. This includes: times, dates, contact people and phone numbers, what to wear, passwords to computers, maps, a list of tasks or expectations—all of the WHO, WHAT, WHEN and WHERE. Unless recorded somewhere in a checklist or computer file, important pieces too easily fall through the cracks when we rely on individual memory alone. Volunteers end up looking or feeling stupid or making mistakes that drive you crazy. More than

---

[35] 1 Peter 5:14, NIV

SECRET #6: *Tap into Built-In Enthusiasm*

likely, because you are human too, you probably blame them. This category may be one of the main culprits for the Volunteer frustration and drop-out.

S – Make sure they have the right **SKILLS** to be successful. You may need to show them, train them, or provide a little on-the-job mentoring. They may be skilled but that does not mean they know all of the ins and outs that make your ministry unique or how you like to have things done.

S – Give them the full **SUPPORT** needed to be successful. This could include: a name badge (first and last name, please), an official logo shirt, keys, computer, office space, cleaning supplies, craft material, songbook, telephone, administrative assistance, or whatever it takes to successfully fulfill the job requirements. Bonus: inform them of any changes in a timely manner. I have heard more than one story of a Volunteer who arrived to work at an event that had been cancelled. Ouch! Just pretend they are being paid. What would an employee need? If an employee needs it to get the job done right, so does your Volunteer.

Use the **K.I.S.S. CHECKLIST** to help you gather the right information to make sure your Volunteers have everything they need to be successful and motivated. See **APPENDIX 6C: *K.I.S.S. CHECKLIST*** to get started. Feel free to add your own logo and data and tweak to fit your circumstances.

Of course, fully equipping workers for service is more expansive than just an orientation or even the initial **K.I.S.S.** On-going training such as growing the skill base of your volunteer team and especially leadership development are important components to consider for your overall volunteer support system. In addition, your leaders will also need to know how to coach, manage conflict, solve problems, manage time and projects effectively and sometimes deal with difficult people (yes, even in churches). And that is just to name a few.

If you are truly committed to 100% engagement, you are going to need a lot of leaders (paid and unpaid) to be running all of those volunteer teams. Volunteers may be free labor, but the required support is not. And without support to ensure successful experiences, Volunteers sooner or later look for the nearest exit.

...without support to ensure successful experiences, Volunteers sooner or later look for the nearest exit.

Consider giving **8½ SECRETS** to your leaders or those you are growing into leadership. This will go a long way toward developing a consistent church-wide approach to *the care and feeding of* your priceless Volunteers.

CONNECT SERVICE TO PASSIONS AND INTERESTS

What are your potential Volunteers passionate about? Do you know? The following three steps will help you get started.

FIRST – THINK ABOUT YOUR PEOPLE (i.e., the entire congregation)

Who are they? Start by looking at their life stages or age groups. What specific activities, hobbies, talents, and interests are associated with any particular age group? What are children interested in? Teens? Senior citizens? Stay-at-home moms? Women? Men? Talking with these age-based groups may uncover their interests and talents and open up untold opportunities for ministry.

- Identify where their interests dovetail with your existing ministries

- Consider expanding your ministry outreach with the new talent you have uncovered

- Compile an on-going list of organizations and opportunities to refer any potential Volunteers whose talents/interests are outside the scope of your mission and vision. *(Just because something is good to do doesn't mean it is right for your organization to do.)*

Here are some ideas that other churches have implemented that originated from Volunteer interest. Scrapbooking might support your Adoption Ministry's *family books* required by adoption agencies. Amateur (or professional) photographers can spearhead the creation of an updated church directory. Older children can support sports and recreation activities for younger children. Grandmas who love to hug babies can support your young moms' MOPS ministry by volunteering as *Rocker Moms* in the nursery. Those (of any age) who have a heart for seniors could plan regular visits to nursing homes to run BINGO sessions or sing-alongs or take their pet along to bring a smile or two. People who love to write could send cards to shut-ins or deployed military men and women. They could also write publicity material or articles for the church newsletter to promote volunteer opportunities or special events. Computer-savvy teens or college students may be the ideal support for your IT department to update your church website to become more user friendly. Crafters can use their talents for costume creation for dramas or decorations for special events. The mechanically-gifted can support your service ministries that help single moms or seniors with car or home repair. Retired business executives and/or administrators can organize and manage short-term projects of every kind—including, perhaps, running the above focus groups to sort out your pool of potential Volunteers. The possibilities are endless if you think first about the untapped treasure that is still *sitting on the benches*.

Just because something is good to do doesn't mean it is right for your organization to do.

We definitely want 100% participation, but not everyone will necessarily match our existing opportunities. It is helpful to be aware of volunteer opportunities available outside of the church to direct a serving-heart in the right direction. God is working everywhere! Volunteering is not limited to our cloistered church opportunities. Just think of the great publicity that will result as they reach out into the community providing helping hands (…perhaps wearing your tee shirt, name badge or just talking about your church as they meet new people).

Spiritual gifts, personality assessments (targeted for faith-based

SECRET #6: *Tap into Built-In Enthusiasm*

populations) and interest/skill inventories are also wonderful tools for helping Volunteers understand how God has prepared them for service. You do not have to reinvent the wheel. There are tons of readily-available resources to assist you. Google away. Or check out Willow Creek Community Church in Chicago and Saddleback Church in Los Angeles as a starting place for your investigation.

SECOND – THINK ABOUT HOW YOU COULD CREATIVELY RESTRUCTURE JOBS

You can expand your Volunteer base by restructuring your tasks to accommodate people who might only be available for short-term commitments—such as your retired *snowbirds* who travel south for the winter. For a more detailed explanation see **SECRET #7:** *Restructure Volunteer Opportunities to Expand Your Volunteer Base*. Do not limit your thinking. You can create projects that require high level responsibility, high level talent and leadership opportunities.

THIRD – (NOTE: Third not First!) THINK ABOUT YOUR EXISTING NEEDS

When our needs are the first thing we focus on, it is easy to get tunnel-vision and become overwhelmed by the urgency of the need. We run the risk of placing the wrong person in the job. If a pulse is the critical qualification, we are probably not looking at the right criteria. Believe it or not, it is better to have no one in a job than have the wrong person. It is much more difficult and time-consuming, in the long run, to get the wrong person out than it is to get the right person in. For one thing, you will not have the damage to undo. Talk about time-consuming and awkward! Most Ministry Leaders I have met have *been there—done that* at least once. Have you ever had to pay that price tag? Pretty high, isn't it?

GIFTING VS. GRUNT WORK

Service is not just about getting the job done. It is also about what God is doing in us. What did God have in mind for your Volunteer when he gifted her with unique talents and passions? Shouldn't she be using these talents on a regular basis? Tony Morgan and Tim Stevens, authors of "Simply Strategic Volunteers: Empowering People for Ministry", addresses this topic in their chapter "Someone Has to Clean the Toilets." [36] They recommend "80 percent of people's time should be spent doing what God has created them to do...the remaining 20 percent of their time should be fulfilling *roles*" (i.e., picking up trash, setting up rooms, cleaning toilets or whatever else needs to be done to make it all work). I worked in more than a few churches where Volunteers have found themselves in *roles* until *the second-coming* or until they quit, exhausted and frustrated. How do your Volunteers fare? It might be worth checking out.

In the corporate arena, this 80/20 Rule is known as the Pareto Principle.[37] It suggests that 80% of business comes from 20% of the customers; 80% of your profit comes from 20% of your product line; 80% of your complaints come from 20% of your customers (or congregation). It looks as if Pastors Morgan and Stevens are suggesting the Pareto Principle applies to churches as well. Is 80% of the Volunteer work done by only 20% of the congregation? Does that sound familiar? Count yourself blessed, if you can claim more than 20% of your congregation actively involved in service—even though we are all called to service. In Ephesians 2:10, we are told that "we are God's masterpiece," and that God has created us "...anew in Christ Jesus, so we can do the good things he planned

---

[36] Tony Morgan and Tim Stevens, *Simply Strategic Volunteers: Empowering People for Ministry*, (Loveland, CO: Group, 2005), 19.

[37] Joseph M. Juran, engineer and management consultant, coined the term "Pareto Principle" in 1941; naming it after Vilfredo Pareto who first observed that most things in life are not distributed evenly (1896).

SECRET #6: *Tap into Built-In Enthusiasm*

for us long ago."[38] Unfortunately, the consumer class is alive and well—and huge—in many churches.

Working in the 80% Zone is an awesome target to shoot for. How good are you at balancing your needs and your Volunteers' passions and interests? I have seen more than my share of 20% passion and 80% grunt work assignments, haven't you? Do you know your current ratio? Start today to make it better. Your Volunteers will love you for it. Not only will it increase their energy and commitment to your ministry work, it will put them right where God wants them to be so he can do his work in them. Another win-win. God's plan is clever that way—again.

Remember that every believer is called to service. The key is embracing the Kingdom Goal: Give everyone (that means 100%) a meaningful opportunity to serve in the areas of their giftedness—spiritual, talent, skill or interest. While you are looking for Volunteers, Volunteers are looking for you. More accurately, they are looking for the right place to serve. Make the right place easier to find...please. This is fixable. Really.

> *The key is embracing the Kingdom Goal:*
> *Give everyone (that means 100%) a meaningful*
> *opportunity to serve in the areas of their*
> *giftedness—spiritual, talent, skill or interest.*

---

[38] Ephesians 2:10, NLT

☑ Action Steps to Tap into Existing Enthusiasm:

☐ 1. Talk to your current Volunteers to better understand their individual motivators. See **APPENDICES 6A-B:** *Motivation Self-Assessment.* See how many motivators you can implement.

☐ 2. Create a Volunteer team of detectives to uncover the hidden obstacles that may still be present in your **PATHWAYS**.

☐ 3. Go for the *biggest bang for the buck*. What can you do quickly to power-up the three **UNIVERSAL MOTIVATORS** that touch almost everybody?

☐ 4. Make a commitment to use the K.I.S.S. CHECKLIST to help every one of your Volunteers to be successful. **See APPENDIX 6C: *K.I.S.S. CHECKLIST***

☐ 5. Go to www.JuneKenny.com for free training Worksheets, helpful tips on working with Volunteers, to participate in discussions and to share your ideas.

SECRET #6: *Tap into Built-In Enthusiasm*

☑ Actions I Plan to Take to Tap Into Existing Enthusiasm:

1._____

2._____

3._____

4._____

5._____

6._____

7._____

8._____

APPENDIX 6A: *Motivation Self-Assessment*

Name_____ Ministry Team_____

Motivation Self-Assessment

We differ in what motivates us. Ministry team members are also motivated by different needs and values.

Read through the following motivators and **CHECK ALL** that apply to you.

- ☐ Friendships/Church "Family"
- ☐ Quality
- ☐ BHAGs *("Big, Hairy, Audacious Goals")*
- ☐ Public Recognition
- ☐ Variety
- ☐ Working in Groups
- ☐ Appreciation
- ☐ Fun & Laughter
- ☐ Competition
- ☐ Action
- ☐ Use Specific Expertise/Skill
- ☐ Challenge
- ☐ Being Included
- ☐ Achievement/Accomplishment
- ☐ Being Needed
- ☐ Predictable Routine
- ☐ Chance to be Creative
- ☐ Casual Recognition ("atta boy")
- ☐ Doing it Right
- ☐ Chance to Make a Difference
- ☐ Chance to Learn
- ☐ Attending Church Conferences
- ☐ Working Alone
- ☐ Other:_____
- ☐ Other:_____
- ☐ Relaxed Environment
- ☐ Being Respected/Valued
- ☐ Food
- ☐ A Leader with Integrity
- ☐ Excitement
- ☐ Freedom/Autonomy
- ☐ A Christian Atmosphere
- ☐ Clarity of Direction, Goals, Tasks
- ☐ Having Responsibility
- ☐ Chance to Express Ideas, Suggestions, Opinions
- ☐ Precision/Accuracy
- ☐ Calm, Even-Paced Environment
- ☐ Opportunities to Lead or Become a Leader
- ☐ A Hug
- ☐ Environment with Little or No Conflict
- ☐ Fast-Paced Environment
- ☐ Clearly Identifiable Results
- ☐ Private Recognition (one-on-one)
- ☐ Working behind the scenes
- ☐ Other:_____
- ☐ Other:_____

My Top Five Motivators

From the list of motivators you have identified above, please select **your personal top five** motivators.

Motivator	Signature
1.	
2.	
3.	
4.	
5.	

APPENDIX 6B: *Motivation Team Activity* DIRECTIONS

Motivation Self-Assessment Directions

1. <u>Training Activity for Leaders</u> (20 min. or 50 min.)
   (What motivates me? What motivates others?)
2. <u>Volunteer Team Activity</u> (25 min.)
   (Why guess? Ask them.)

MATERIALS:
One "Motivation Self-Assessment" handout per participant
3-5 Prizes (Candy or inexpensive fun items)
Flip chart paper for Brainstorm activity (optional)

ACTIVITY:

"What Motivates Me? What Motivates Others?"
(Leader Version)

Training Activity for Leaders:
Part I = 20 min./Part II = 30 min. Total = 50 min.
Part I: Assessment + Signature Contest

Step #1: (5 min.) Distribute Self-Assessment Handout to each person to complete.

SETUP SCRIPT:

*"Ephesians 6:7 tells us to 'Work with enthusiasm, as though you were working for the Lord rather than people.' God obviously wants us to be energetic and motivated in all the work we do. I know we would like to be able to do that all the time, but how? How does one manage to stay motivated? What gets us excited about a project or task? Today we have an opportunity to get a clearer picture of what kinds of things motivate each of us. Here is a list of over 40 motivators. Please quickly check **ALL** that*

APPENDIX 6B: *Motivation Team Activity* DIRECTIONS

personally inspire or energize you—whether at work, at home, in volunteer situations—anywhere. This should only take 2-3 minutes."

*Do not give additional directions until everyone is ready to proceed with Step #2.

Step #2: (1-2 min.)
SETUP SCRIPT:
*"Now, select the **FIVE most important ones to you** and write them in the spaces at the bottom of the page. When you are finished, I am going to ask you to do something fun with that information."*

Step #3: (6 min.)
SETUP SCRIPT:
*"Is everyone ready? We are going to have a little contest. **You will have 5 minutes** to acquire as many signatures as possible. In order for people to sign your sheet, they must also have selected one of your motivators in their **TOP 5 LIST**. But they may only sign your sheet once, matching one motivator. You will need five different signatures. Just to make it interesting, I have prizes for the first ____(#) that acquire all 5 signatures. What questions do you have before we begin?"*

Step #4: (7 min.) DEBRIEF
    a. People return to seats (1 minute)
    b. Give out prizes (1 minute)
    c. Discuss: (5 minutes)
- "What Observations did you make?" (get their responses first)
- "Did anyone have a motivator that no one else seemed to have?"

APPENDIX 6B: *Motivation Team Activity* DIRECTIONS

(Ask: "Does anyone here have the 'missing' motivator?" Do this for as many of the missing motivators as you have time. Have fun with this. People like to find others that are motivated by the same things—especially the unusual ones.)

KEY LEARNING POINTS:
"My motivators are not universal motivators."
"Some people are actually motivated by things that I would avoid."
This is usually an "aha" moment for some leaders.

FOR LEADERS: Leaders often make the mistake of only including the motivators that appeal to them. When in doubt about what your Volunteers want, ask them.
How can you provide some of the motivators that have just been uncovered?

Training Activity for Leaders:
Part I = 20 min./Part II = 30 min. Total = 50 min.
Part II: How Do We Include More Motivators in Our Ministry?

Step #5: (5 min.) Create table discussion groups of 4-6 people each. Assign each group 1-2 motivators. Or work with the motivators your team has identified as important.
SETUP SCRIPT:
"How might we creatively incorporate these motivators into our work/tasks/goals?"
"We have _____ minutes to work, so you might want to select 2-3 that seem important to your group. Come up with as many ideas as you can for each."

Step #6: (10 min.) Groups brainstorm creative ways to incorporate

APPENDIX 6B: *Motivation Team Activity* DIRECTIONS

motivators into ministry. Flip charts can capture best ideas.

Step #7: (10 min.) Groups Report Out Best Ideas (2 minutes each) "What ideas did you have?"

Step #8: (5 min.) Decide on NEXT STEPS
Some Ideas:
  a. Identify a committee to create action plan(s) on one or more ideas and report back.
  b. **Or,** put on next meeting's agenda for team to create specific action plan(s).
  c. **Or,** one member volunteers to type up all the ideas and circulate list to team members. Team members individually vote their choice for the **five best ideas**. They return their data to the coordinator who consolidates the results for the leader. The leader receives a ranked list of the **ten most important motivators** for the team as a whole.
  d. **Or, Identify What Motivates Your Volunteers.** Leaders can use the following activity with their teams to identify the specific key motivators of each team member. Then leader designs projects and tasks with specific motivators in mind based on individual assignments.

ACTIVITY:
"What Motivates Me? What Motivates Others?"
(Volunteer Version)

> **Volunteer Team Activity: Total = 25 min.**
> **Teambuilding for Volunteer Team /**
> **Valuable Information for Leader**

Step #1: (5 min.) Distribute Self-Assessment Handout to each person to complete.

APPENDIX 6B: *Motivation Team Activity* DIRECTIONS

SETUP SCRIPT:
*"Ephesians 6:7 tells us to 'Work with enthusiasm, as though you were working for the Lord rather than people.' God obviously wants us to be energetic and motivated in all the work we do. I know we would like to be able to do that all the time, but how? How does one manage to stay motivated? What gets us excited about a project or task? Today we have an opportunity to get a clearer picture of what kinds of things motivate each of us. Here is a list of over 40 motivators. Please check **ALL that personally inspire or energize you**—whether at work, at home, in volunteer situations—anywhere. This should only take 2-3 minutes."*

*Do not give additional directions until everyone is ready to proceed with Step #2.

Step #2: (1-2 min.)
SETUP SCRIPT:
*"Now, select the **FIVE most important ones to you** and write them in the spaces at the bottom of the page."*

Step #3: (6-8 min.) Each person shares their top motivators with the team.

Step #4: (10 min.)
DISCUSS: Common motivators? Unusual motivators?
Ask: *"How can we incorporate some of these motivators in the way we do ministry?"* Have someone record the ideas generated.

AFTER — **Step #5:** Leaders use this activity with their teams to identify the specific key motivators of each team member. Then the leader designs projects and tasks with specific motivators in mind based on individual assignments.

141

APPENDIX 6C: *K.I.S.S. CHECKLIST*

K.I.S.S. CHECKLIST for every
<u>NEW VOLUNTEER</u>

added to the _____ Ministry
(NAME)

Team/Project:

If you Love your Volunteers, Greet them with a K.I.S.S.

1 Peter 5:14, NIV
"Greet one another with the kiss of love."

Almost <u>UNIVERSAL MOTIVATORS</u>

Volunteers want:
- To know and be known
- To be part of something bigger than themselves
- To make a positive difference somewhere for someone

<u>Goal of a Great Ministry Leader:</u>

- Help each and every Volunteer successfully make a positive difference. (Note: this translates directly to your ministry or project success, too.)
- Help Volunteers recognize the God-sized impact that can happen even in the most mundane of tasks.
- Help them to meet and bond with others on your team "to know and be known".
- Help them to identify with _____ Church as a member of "the something bigger" so that every victory becomes a shared victory.

APPENDIX 6C: *K.I.S.S. CHECKLIST*

- Incorporate the 3 Universal Motivators with a Christian K.I.S.S. and you will go a long way in achieving this goal.

☐ Create an online Ministry Information Folder that can be accessed by Ministry Leaders.

(✶) Indicates that this item can be accessed

☐ PRINT documents to-be-shared with a new Volunteer, EMAIL individual documents or SEND LINK to the accessible file called **"NEW Volunteer Info"** file—whatever works best for your ministry/project operation. The important thing is to get this information into the hands of your Volunteer.

APPENDIX 6C: *K.I.S.S. CHECKLIST*

K.I.S.S. CHECKLIST for every
<u>NEW VOLUNTEER</u>

added to the _____ Ministry
(NAME)

Team/Project:

K – <u>Kingdom Impact</u>:

1. ☐ Explain/describe the Kingdom Impact of your specific Ministry or project-at-hand (i.e., how it specifically touches others with the love of Christ and/or makes a positive difference).

2. ☐ Connect SPECIFIC TASKS to Kingdom Impact—show how these tasks contribute to ministry success.

3. ☐ Other: _____

I – <u>Information</u>:

1. ☐ Discuss LENGTH of TIME commitment, RESPONSIBILITIES and specific GOALS of the Ministry or project.

2. ☐ Personally Introduce New Volunteer to each member of ministry or project team.

3. ☐ Assign *Go-To Support Person* for each NEW Volunteer for a specified time period (example: 3 months/duration of project/etc.). Provide Contact Information (phone #/text #/email) to both.

APPENDIX 6C: *K.I.S.S. CHECKLIST*

4. ☐ (✽) **OPTIONAL:** provide contact information (phone #/text #/email) of entire team. (NOTE: This will make **interaction** and **potential Volunteer-driven "substitution"** more accessible).

5. ☐ (✽) List of ALL future scheduled committee **MEETING** and/or **EVENT** times and dates.

6. ☐ (✽) Copy of _____'s **BEHAVIORAL COVENANT** (to read and sign).

7. ☐ Other: _____

S – **Skills Needed:** (if appropriate, provide training)

1. ☐ Other: _____

2. ☐ Other: _____

S – **Support:**

1. ☐ *(Possibilities: Name Badge, Church Logo Shirt, etc.)*

2. ☐ *(Possibilities: Materials, Keys, Equipment, etc.)*

3. ☐ Provide **Go-To Support Person** to assist Volunteer in initial stages of ministry/project in order to provide orientation, introductions and be available on an *on-going basis* for questions, etc.

APPENDIX 6C: *K.I.S.S. CHECKLIST*

4. ☐ **OPTIONAL:** Provide *shadowing, first-serve, test-drive* ministry experience to introduce new Volunteer to ministry—a *Taste & See* experience.

5. ☐ Check back with Volunteer at conclusion of introductory period or end of project to assess the experience. ASK the following:
    - How did the Volunteer feel about the experience?
    - Was it a good fit?
    - Would they like to continue in this ministry or sample another?
    - What did they learn in the process that they *wished they had known* at the beginning?
    - Etc.

    (Use this information to improve the orientation process.)

6. ☐ Other: _____

#7: Restructure Volunteer Opportunities to Expand Your Volunteer Base

So, how do we do that?

It is frustrating to be continually short-handed. It is equally frustrating for potential Volunteers to want to help but unable to accommodate what you are asking (i.e., your job design). For example, think of the young mother with a toddler at home. She may have excellent administrative skills, want to use those skills to help, but simply cannot make a commitment to show up every Tuesday from 9-11 a.m.—even if you provide the gift of child care. Children get sick—frequently. The problem is not the Volunteer. The problem is not your administrative need. The problem is the job design. Expand your job designs and you will expand your Volunteer pool. Period.

You may have mountains of jobs to be done, but if they are all the same kind of job, you are unnecessarily narrowing the volume of Volunteers who can comply with your job requirements. In this chapter you will discover how to:

1) Analyze the kinds of opportunities you are actually offering your Volunteers.
2) Uncover which of the eight job categories might be an untapped resource for you.
3) Restructure some of your existing jobs to fit those untapped categories and attract more Volunteers.

You may be asking, "Why should I restructure my jobs? These are the jobs I need done." Okay, that is a fair question. The answer is that you have somewhere between 60-80% of your people still *sitting on the bench*. By restructuring your volunteer opportunities, more of your unused Volunteers (a.k.a., the 60-80%) will be available and eager to help. People want to serve. See **SECRET #6: *Tap into Built-In Enthusiasm.*** As a leader, you want them to serve. "He that thinketh he leadeth, and hath no one following him, is only taking a walk."[39] And God wants them to serve.[40] By restructuring your jobs—at least some of them—you will have the potential to create a win-win-win situation.

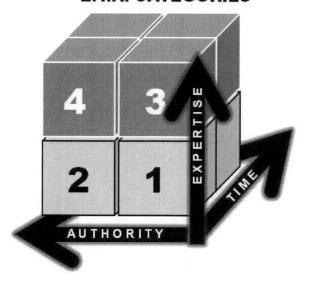

8 VOLUNTEER OPPORTUNITY E.T.A. CATEGORIES

Understanding how your current jobs are designed can produce a major breakthrough in expanding your Volunteer base. How? You will discover not only where your current jobs are, you will discover where they are not. Each job is designed with three important characteristics:

---

[39] John Maxwell, pastor and author of *The 5 Levels of Leadership: Proven Steps to Maximize Your Potential* and over 60 other leadership books.
[40] Ephesians 2:10

SECRET #7: *Restructure Volunteer Opportunities to Expand Your Volunteer Base*

- **EXPERTISE (E)**
- **TIME Commitment (T)**
- **AUTHORITY (A)**

Since every job has all three characteristics, each job fits into one of the eight distinct **E.T.A.** Categories. If you identify the **E.T.A.** of your current volunteer opportunities, you will know exactly how many are in each category. More importantly, you will discover which of the eight categories are under-used. It is entirely possible that the lack of participation is not due to lack of motivation at all, but to the job's design. Good news! This is fixable. If a category is underused, simply redesign some of your existing jobs to fit that category as well as its existing category. This opens the door to new Volunteers.

It is entirely possible that the lack of participation is not due to lack of motivation at all, but to the job's design.

So what exactly is an **E.T.A.** rating and how do I determine what is what?

The "E" stands for level of **EXPERTISE** needed to do the job. Ask yourself, "Is this a task that anyone could do?" "Could it be taught quickly or successfully achieved using programmed materials?" If so, it would be classified as **LOWER EXPERTISE** because almost anyone could fit the bill. On the other hand, if it is critical that the Volunteer arrive with a well-developed specific skill set, such as computer knowledge, musical gifts or high-level administrative experience, it would be classified as **HIGHER**

149

EXPERTISE.

The "T" stands for **TIME Commitment**. What is the long-term duration of the expected time commitment? Short-term can be one day, one event, a single time slot of service or even several months of intense work. It does not matter if the job itself takes thirty minutes or three hours at a time. You want to clarify how long you want that Volunteer to commit to do that thirty-minute or three-hour job. Okay, who are we kidding? You really want the Volunteer to commit to that job until the Second Coming. Unfortunately, that unrealistic leadership expectation is one of the things that prevents Volunteers from raising their hands in the first place. If you want them to commit to serving as a greeter for thirty minutes, two Sundays a month for a year, by definition, it is a **LONGER TERM** job **(E.T.A. #5-6-7-8)**. If you want them to commit to three hours of hospitality service and clean-up at a single event, it is a **SHORTER TERM** job **(E.T.A. #1-2-3-4)**. Here is an easy way to tell the difference. Short-term jobs have a defined end date or a specific completion point. Long-term jobs are usually a commitment of a year or more with on-going repetitive responsibilities.

The "A" stands for the level of **AUTHORITY** required. Do you need someone who will organize and run an event, ministry, department, or someone who will just perform the tasks? Some jobs require team leaders and project organizers, a **HIGH level of AUTHORITY (EVEN #s E.T.A. #2-4-6-8)**, while others need team members and workers, a **LOW level of AUTHORITY (ODD #s E.T.A. #1-3-5-7)**.

Here are the eight distinct categories at your disposal based on these three characteristics:

8 VOLUNTEER OPPORTUNITY E.T.A. CATEGORIES

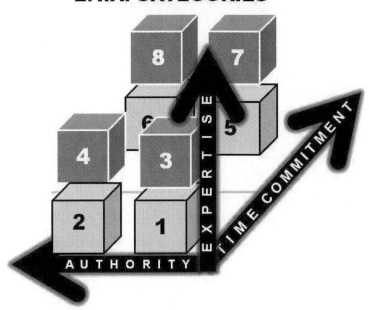

KEY

Lower #s = shorter time
Higher #s = longer time

Odd #s = Team Members
Even #s = Team Leaders

Lighter Cubes = Lower Expertise Needed
Darker Cubes = Higher Expertise Needed

Are you utilizing all eight? Probably not. Do you think you might have more participation if you were? Let us go out on a limb and say "yes!"

STEP ONE: DETERMINE WHERE YOU ARE NOW

It is difficult to know where to expand until we know where we are now. Ask yourself, "What specific jobs, tasks or projects do I need to have done to make my ministry work?" Make a list. A big list. Pretend you had the luxury of being able to delegate each and every job to someone who was dying to do it. Even if you would like to keep some of the choice jobs for yourself, pretend you had to temporarily hand them off. All of them. What would you include on your ministry list? Be creative. Be comprehensive. And be sure to include jobs that demand high-level expertise and major responsibilities. Volunteers will do these things for you if you give them the opportunity.

For ideas, check out **APPENDIX 1C:** *Case Study* to see a list of the different kinds of jobs required to run a MOPS ministry. Hint: do not think about the individual people. Think about the jobs that need to be done: childcare, registration, presentations, set up, clean up, hospitality, publicity, etc. A single Volunteer may be doing multiple jobs for you. That can get confusing. By thinking about the tasks to be done, you will find it easier to get your arms around what work actually goes into successfully achieving your ministry goals. Once the tasks are clear, it will be easier for you to combine and repackage those tasks in a way that will allow others to participate in God's work too.

SECRET #7: Restructure Volunteer Opportunities to Expand Your Volunteer Base

To help you expand your lists, consider each of the following sub-groups:

- **Higher Expertise (E.T.A. Categories #3-4-7-8)**
  What jobs require some sort of higher expertise, skill or talent?

- **Lower Expertise (E.T.A. Categories #1-2-5-6)**
  What opportunities do you offer that anyone could easily learn to do or easily accomplish using programmed materials?

- **Lower Authority/Team Member or Worker (E.T.A. Categories #1-3-5-7)**
  What jobs need anyone and everyone to get the job done? (team member positions)

- **Higher Authority/Team Leader or Coordinator (E.T.A. Categories #2-4-6-8)**
  Where are you currently offering leadership opportunities? Where could you use someone to help you get organized?

- **Shorter Term Commitments (E.T.A. Categories #1-2-3-4)**
  Note: a single event or a job with a specific completion point (i.e., a project).

- **Longer Term Commitments (E.T.A. Categories #5-6-7-8)**
  Note: usually a commitment of a year or more with on-going repetitive responsibilities.

8½ SECRETS

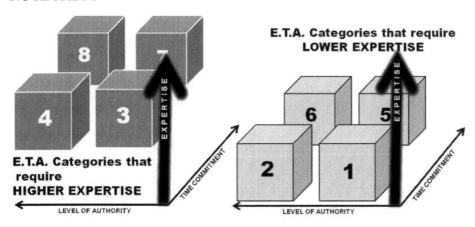

Higher Expertise Jobs: *(Note: Specialized skills required)*	**Lower Expertise Jobs:** *(Note: Skills quickly learned)*

SECRET #7: *Restructure Volunteer Opportunities to Expand Your Volunteer Base*

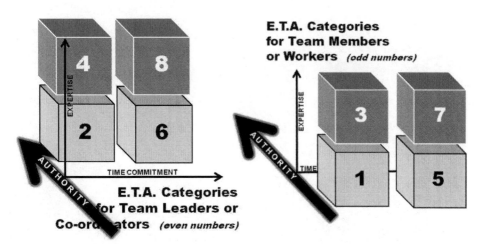

Team Leader/Organizer Jobs:	Team Member/Worker Jobs:
(Note: Leadership = even numbers)	*(Note: Workers = odd numbers)*

8½ SECRETS

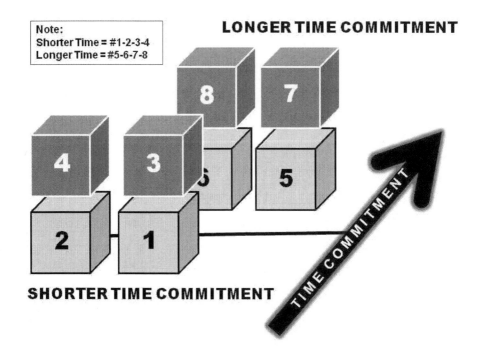

Once you have your list of jobs/tasks/positions that make your ministry work, proceed to step two.

STEP TWO: IDENTIFY THE E.T.A. OF EACH CURRENT JOB OR VOLUNTEER OPPORTUNITY

You can easily identify the **E.T.A.** of each of your jobs or positions by asking three questions.

Question #1: What is the level of EXPERTISE needed?

- ↑ **HIGHER (E)** – The job needs a specific skill or talent to do the job—something not easily trained by us. (Examples: web design skills, musical skills, high-level experience or credentials.)
- ↓ **LOWER (E)** – The job may need basic people skills and communication skills but

the specific skills needed can easily be trained by us or we will provide materials that will ensure success. (Examples: ushers, nursery care workers, greeters, church set-up and clean-up crews, etc.)

Question #2: What is the TIME Commitment?

⬆ **HIGHER (T)** – The job requires a longer term commitment with on-going responsibilities or tasks—usually a year or more is expected.

⬇ **LOWER (T)** – The job is a project, event or limited task—i.e., any task that has a beginning, middle and end (e.g., Annual Men's Breakfast or ad hoc team to revise the web site). Difficulty can be high or low and can require a few hours to several months.

Question #3: What is the level of AUTHORITY?

⬆ **HIGHER (A)** – Think of a team leader or coordinator with high responsibility for planning or organizing in addition to overseeing the task. (Example: Wednesday night dinner co-coordinator.)

⬇ **LOWER (A)** – Think of a team member or worker responsible for tasks but not responsible for managing or leading others. (Example: Choir member.)

You can use **APPENDIX 7A Directions** to help you get organized. Circle "HIGHER" or "LOWER" in each of the three columns on **APPENDIX 7B Worksheet.** Use **APPENDIX 7C:**

E.T.A. Identification Tool to determine the correct category. You can also go to www.JuneKenny.com to download a free Microsoft Excel file that has been programmed to automatically identify your **E.T.A. Categories** for you. Just type in the job name, indicate the level of Expertise, Time and Authority, and PRESTO! the **E.T.A. Category** will appear. This will be helpful too when you want to create a separate list for each type of job. Just select the "SORT" option and print.

ANALYZE YOUR CURRENT VOLUNTEER OPPORTUNITIES

Directions: Indicate the Level of EXPERTISE needed, Level of TIME Commitment and AUTHORITY Level by selecting LOWER or HIGHER (in drop-down boxes). ETA Category will automatically be assigned.

#	VOLUNTEER POSITION:	Expertise	Time	Authority	ETA Category
1	Greeter	Lower	Higher	Lower	5
2	Church Chairman	Higher	Higher	Higher	8
3	Video Team Member	Higher	Higher	Lower	7
4	Video Team Leader	Higher	Higher	Higher	8
5	Nursery Helper	Lower	Higher	Lower	5
6	Greeter Co-ordinator	Lower	Higher	Higher	6
7	Spring Clean-Up Vol.	Lower	Lower	Lower	1
8	Christmas Musical Prog.	Higher	Lower	Lower	3
9	Choir Member	Higher	Higher	Lower	7
10	Church Nurse	Higher	Higher	Higher	8
11	Fall Clean-Up Co-Ord.	Lower	Lower	Higher	2
12	Conf.Co-Ordinator	Higher	Lower	Higher	4

Once you have identified your existing jobs by asking the above three questions, you will be able to get a much better picture of how your current ministry opportunities are structured.

STEP THREE: CREATE A SEPARATE LIST FOR EACH TYPE OF JOB (i.e., 8 E.T.A. Categories)

See **APPENDICES 7D-L:** *Individual E.T.A. Categories.* Note: you can easily print individual lists from the downloaded Excel file. These lists will tell you exactly how many jobs are in each of the eight categories. The bonus: you will also find three or more categories that have fewer workers. Ask yourself if some of the jobs in the more-populated categories could also be restructured to fit the less-populated ones. The key word here is "also." You can keep the job in both categories.

STEP FOUR: BRAINSTORM JOBS THAT COULD FIT IN EACH OF THE UNDER-USED CATEGORIES

Start with any current jobs that can be restructured to fit in any of the under-used categories. Notice I did not suggest that you eliminate any current jobs—only expand them to fit into multiple categories.

HINT: For a *fast start* on restructuring your jobs: Only TIME is flexible. EXPERTISE and **AUTHORITY** typically do not change. **Start by expanding your E.T.A. #2, #3 & #4 Categories.** Can you think of ways to restructure a particular task into a shorter time commitment or project? By "project" I mean anything that has a beginning, middle and an end. Events are projects. Pulling weeds on a Saturday is a project. Volunteering for a one-week Vacation Bible School is a project. A Christmas program, redesigning your website, fixing a single mom's car and baking a cake for a funeral luncheon also qualify.

I imagine there is some frustration out there right about now. "I have a hard enough time filling these positions once. Are you

159

8½ SECRETS

asking me to find multiple people to do the same tasks?" Yes! Exactly! Maybe the reason you are having such difficulty is that the people *on the bench* cannot promise you a year or two. For example, a Michigan retiree who spends the winter in Florida might be able to promise you three or four months in the spring and summer, but nothing in the fall and winter. Possibly someone else would like to try a new volunteer position and might be willing to commit short term in order to be able to test the waters. (And <u>be able to quit without guilt</u> if it does not work out.) Just because a job may be on-going does not mean the person has to be. Besides, you can be creative here. Why not create another job – the person who will recruit and manage the team of short-termers for that specific project? This position can be long term (**E.T.A. #6 or #8**) or short term (**E.T.A. #2 or #4**). Restructuring jobs with shorter time commitments (including higher authority/leadership jobs) will definitely expand opportunities to your current *bench-warmers* who would love to serve **(see SECRET #6:** *Tap into Built-In Enthusiasm***).**

Can you imagine what would happen if you used all eight? Simply design the jobs to fit into multiple categories and make them more accessible to those who may have been left out in the past due to time constraints.

STEP FIVE: GET TOGETHER WITH YOUR TEAM TO BRAINSTORM WHICH JOBS CAN BE MORE EASILY RESTRUCTURED

Start with all of the longer term jobs: **E.T.A. Categories #5-6-7-8**. How can they be turned into projects with defined end dates or completion points: **E.T.A. Categories #1-2-3-4**. Be creative and design project-based jobs. It is not my goal to create more work for you. I am passionate about helping you share your load. Ministry burnout is real! Let more Volunteers help you—with everything!

The under-used potential Volunteers are sitting there waiting for you. Anyone and everyone could serve, if the opportunity matched the time and the talent. "If you think [someone is] too small to be effective, you have never been in bed with a mosquito."[41] Even children can be involved in God's work as contributors—not just consumers. Dr. Martin Luther King, Jr. understood the power and empowerment of 100% participation. "Everybody can be great because anybody can serve. [They] don't have to have a college degree to serve. [They] don't have to make their subject and verb agree to serve. [They] don't have to know the second theory of thermodynamics in physics to serve. [They] only need a heart full of grace. A soul generated by love."[42]

I once heard a pastor sum it up nicely, "The only ability God really cares about is our availability."

Shouldn't that be our perspective as well?

---

[41] Betty Reese, American officer and pilot. *Leadership: A Publication of Christianity Today* (Carol Stream, IL), vol. 16, no. 2, Spring 1995, p. 67.
[42] Dr. Martin Luther King, Jr.

☑ Action Steps to Expand Opportunities:

☐ 1. Analyze your current Volunteer opportunities to determine where you can expand to reach more Volunteers. Use **APPENDICES 7A-L** to help you get organized.

☐ 2. Create a new Volunteer team (comprised of **E.T.A. #1-2-3-4** positions) to do ACTION STEP #1 for you. ☺

☐ 3. Encourage each ministry area to have at least one (more is better) short-term **(E.T.A. #1-2-3-4)** Volunteer job as a *test drive* for Volunteers who might like to try a new serving experience without the usual feelings of guilt or failure if it does not work out.

☐ 4. Go to www.JuneKenny.com to download free PDF Worksheets and a free Microsoft Excel file programmed to analyze your **E.T.A. Categories** automatically.

SECRET #7: *Restructure Volunteer Opportunities to Expand Your Volunteer Base*

☑ Actions I Plan to Take to Expand Opportunities:

1._____

2._____

3._____

4._____

5._____

6._____

7._____

8._____

APPENDIX 7A: *Analyze Volunteer Opportunities* – DIRECTIONS

Analyze Volunteer Opportunities – Directions

Step One: Make a list of your current Volunteer Opportunities.

Step Two: Analyze the job structure (E.T.A.) by asking three questions about each job/task or position.

| FIRST QUESTION | What is the level of **EXPERTISE** needed?

HIGHER (E↑) – The job needs a specific skill/talent – not easily trained by us (example web design skills, musical skills, high-level experience or credentials).

LOWER (E↓) – The job may need basic people skills and/or communication skills, but specific skills for the job can be easily trained by us or we will provide materials that will ensure success.

| SECOND QUESTION | What is the **TIME Commitment**?

HIGHER (T↑) – The job requires a longer term commitment with on-going responsibilities or tasks – usually one year or more.

LOWER (T↓) – The job is a project, event or limited task – i.e., any task that has a beginning, middle and end. Difficulty can be high or low and can require a few hours to several months.

APPENDIX 7A: *Analyze Volunteer Opportunities* DIRECTIONS

> **THIRD QUESTION** — What is **the level of <u>AUTHORITY</u>**?

HIGHER (A⬆) – Think of a team leader or co-coordinator with high responsibility for planning or organization in addition to overseeing the task and workers.

LOWER (A⬇) – Think of a team member or worker responsible for tasks but not responsible for managing or leading others.

Identify the correct E.T.A. categories by using APPENDIX 7B Worksheet and **APPENDIX 7C:** *Identification Tool.* Or go to www.JuneKenny.com to download a free Excel file to identify E.T.A. Categories automatically.

Step Three: Expand Volunteer Opportunities by expanding under-used E.T.A. Job Categories

1. Tally the number of jobs/positions in each of the eight E.T.A. Categories. See **APPENDICES 7D-L**.

2. Determine which categories are currently under-used in your church or ministry.

3. Start by restructuring jobs in categories **#5-6-7-8 (T⬆)** by **ALTERING the TIME commitment.** Which jobs can be redesigned as self-contained projects or events which would allow them to fit into categories **#1-2-3-4 (T⬇)**? Projects can be BIG, but still have a clear end date or completion point. Look to expand categories **#3** and **#4**, especially with retirees in mind.

4. Also, look at the higher authority **(A⬆)** categories **(#2-4-6-8)** to see if you can expand leadership opportunities.

165

APPENDIX 7B: *Analyze Volunteer Opportunities* WORKSHEET

Analyze Volunteer Opportunities – Worksheet

Directions: Circle your answer. Use Chart (Appendix 7: C – "E.T.A. Identification Tool") to identify correct category.*

Task/Job/Position	(E) EXPERTISE		(T) TIME		(A) AUTHORITY		E.T.A. CATEGORY
	HIGHER H	LOWER L	HIGHER H	LOWER L	HIGHER H	LOWER L	
	H	L	H	L	H	L	
	H	L	H	L	H	L	
	H	L	H	L	H	L	
	H	L	H	L	H	L	
	H	L	H	L	H	L	
	H	L	H	L	H	L	
	H	L	H	L	H	L	
	H	L	H	L	H	L	
	H	L	H	L	H	L	

*Or, go to www.JuneKerry.com to download a free Excel file to identify E.T.A. categories automatically.

APPENDIX 7C: *Analyze Volunteer Opportunities* IDENTIFICATION TOOL

Analyze Volunteer Opportunities – E.T.A. Identification Tool

See directions in Appendix 7: A.

EXPERTISE Question #1: Level of Expertise?	TIME Question #2: Time Commitment?	AUTHORITY Question #3: Level of Authority?	FINAL E.T.A. CATEGORY
HIGHER (3 – 4 – 7 – 8)	HIGHER (5–6–7–8)	HIGHER (5–8)	#8
		LOWER (7–8)	#7
	LOWER (3–4)	HIGHER (3–4)	#4
		LOWER (3–4)	#3
LOWER (1 – 2 – 5 – 6)	HIGHER (5–6–7–8)	HIGHER (5–6)	#6
		LOWER (5–6)	#5
	LOWER (1–2–3–4)	HIGHER (1–2)	#2
		LOWER (1–2)	#1

*Or, go to www.JuneKenny.com to download a free Excel file to identify E.T.A. categories automatically.

APPENDIX 7D: *ETA #1*

Expertise **LOWER** /
Time Commitment **LOWER** /
Authority **LOWER**

(i.e., team member or worker for a shorter term project or event.)

VOLUNTEER OPPORTUNITIES:

_____
_____
_____
_____
_____
_____
_____
_____
_____
_____
_____

APPENDIX 7E: *ETA #2*

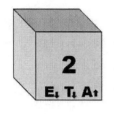

Expertise **LOWER** /
Time Commitment **LOWER** /
Authority **HIGHER**

(i.e., team leader or organizer for a shorter term project or event.)

VOLUNTEER OPPORTUNITIES:

_____
_____
_____
_____
_____
_____
_____
_____
_____
_____

APPENDIX 7F: *ETA #3*

Expertise **HIGHER** /
Time Commitment **LOWER** /
Authority **LOWER**

(i.e., highly skilled team member or worker with a specific expertise committed to a shorter term project or event.)

VOLUNTEER OPPORTUNITIES:

_____

_____

_____

_____

_____

_____

_____

_____

_____

_____

_____

APPENDIX 7G: *ETA #4*

Expertise **HIGHER** /
Time Commitment **LOWER** /
Authority **HIGHER**

(i.e., highly skilled team leader or organizer with a specific expertise committed to a shorter term project or event.)

VOLUNTEER OPPORTUNITIES:

_____

_____

_____

_____

_____

_____

_____

_____

_____

_____

APPENDIX 7H: *ETA #5*

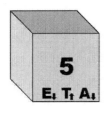

Expertise **LOWER** /
Time Commitment **HIGHER** /
Authority **LOWER**
(i.e., team member or worker involved in on-going, repetitive ministry work and committed for a year or more.)

VOLUNTEER OPPORTUNITIES:

_____
_____
_____
_____
_____
_____
_____
_____
_____
_____
_____

APPENDIX 7J: *ETA #6*

Expertise **LOWER** /
Time Commitment **HIGHER** /
Authority **HIGHER**

(i.e., team leader or organizer involved in on-going, repetitive ministry work and committed for a year or more.)

VOLUNTEER OPPORTUNITIES:

_____

_____

_____

_____

_____

_____

_____

_____

_____

_____

_____

APPENDIX 7K: *ETA #7*

Expertise **HIGHER** /
Time Commitment **HIGHER** /
Authority **LOWER**

(i.e., highly skilled worker or team member with a specific expertise involved in on-going, repetitive ministry work and committed for a year or more.)

VOLUNTEER OPPORTUNITIES:

_____
_____
_____
_____
_____
_____
_____
_____
_____
_____
_____
_____

APPENDIX 7L: *ETA #8*

Expertise **HIGHER** /
Time Commitment **HIGHER** /
Authority **HIGHER**
(i.e., highly skilled team leader or organizer with a specific expertise involved in on-going, repetitive ministry work and committed for a year or more.)

VOLUNTEER OPPORTUNITIES:

_____

_____

_____

_____

_____

_____

_____

_____

_____

_____

 **#8: Lead with Humility— Listen More, Talk Less**

So, how do we do that?

"Listen to advice and accept instruction
that you may gain wisdom in the future."[43]
"Iron sharpens iron, so one person sharpens another."[44]

Of all of the strategies included in this book, **Leading with Humility** is probably the most important one. Why do I say that? Jesus chose that strategy for His mission. He told us. He showed us. After Jesus washed the feet of His disciples, He said,

> Do you understand what I have done for you? ...You call me "Teacher" and "Lord," and rightly so, for that is what I am. Now that I, your Lord and Teacher, have washed your feet, *you also should wash one another's feet. I have set you an example that you should do as I have done for you.* Very truly I tell you, no servant is greater than his master, nor is a messenger greater than the one who sent him. Now that you know these things, *you will be blessed if you do them.*[45]

"For all those who exalt themselves will be humbled, and those who humble themselves will be exalted."[46] To get that kind of biblical attention, humility might just be a big deal after all.

---

[43] Proverbs 19:20, ESV
[44] Proverbs 27:17, NIV
[45] John 13:12-17, NIV *(emphasis mine)*
[46] Luke 14:11, NIV

Even in the corporate sector, humility is beginning to be recognized as a strong leadership approach worth considering. Ken Blanchard, management guru and Christian businessman, introduced his highly acclaimed <u>Leadership by the Book: Tools to Transform Your Workplace</u> in which he proclaimed Jesus Christ as the leader that corporate leaders should emulate. Humility leads to strong leadership? Sound counter-intuitive? It is. God does not think the way we do. Is it really so strange to think this might be the best model for us as well?

If you have made it this far in the book, you are more than likely already a leader of somebody—which means you have intentionally or intuitively decided your leadership approach. What kind of leader have you chosen to be? Can you describe your approach? If you are not sure, simply ask yourself these two questions: "What is my honest opinion of my Volunteers?" and "Where do I place them on the continuum from Grunt Workers to Partners in Ministry?" Your answer will say more about you than them. It reveals your approach to leadership. Are you truly committed to following Christ's model of being a servant leader? The leader who washes feet? The leader whose main job is helping (translate: serving) those he leads to be outrageously successful? A servant leader knows a big secret. Volunteers who succeed result in ministries that succeed. And surprise, it also results in leaders who succeed. If you already see yourself as a servant leader, you are well on your path to becoming a great leader.

Servant leadership is an intentional mindset of choice. To many it seems counter-intuitive or even weak. As a result, this kind of leadership rarely happens by accident. When we intentionally make it part of our church culture, more people will want to *get off the bench* and *into the game*. Many churches have already taken the time to clarify their guiding principles (a.k.a., mindset of choice) for how they intend to support and relate to their Volunteers. Note: this does not mean they are necessarily doing these things right

SECRET #8: *Lead with Humility—Listen More, Talk Less*

now. They intend to do them from now on. This creates the foundation for a church-wide consistent approach for supporting Volunteers—over time becoming an invisible yet integral part of the church culture.

SAMPLE GUIDING PRINCIPLES

Do any of these resonate with your current church culture? Which ones might you want to add?

1. God calls <u>every Christian</u> to utilize his or her talents or gifts in God's work, which means our real goal is 100% participation.[47]

2. Serving is as vital to spiritual growth as breathing is to life.[48]

3. Serving is both a privilege and a blessing.[49]

4. Leading is both a privilege and a blessing.[50]

5. We follow Christ's model of servant leadership[51] by helping others to experience the joy of serving in the center of God's will.

6. Volunteers are our Partners in Ministry (i.e., not our underlings).[52]

7. Volunteers are respected, valued, supported and treated with loving care <u>all of the time</u>. Period. (P.S. This also

---

[47] Ephesians 2:10
[48] James 2:14-17
[49] Genesis 12:2
[50] Luke 14:11, NIV
[51] John 13:12-17
[52] 1 Corinthians 12:12-27

applies to paid staff.)[53]

8. We make it incredibly easy to get connected to serve at

   _____.

   (your church name)

9. Everyone is a connector—even other Volunteers. Most of the time they are the BEST connectors.

10. Excellence in everything we do honors God and inspires people.[54]

11. Others?

What could your church look like if you made a commitment to some or all of these guiding principles?

Do not be distressed if these principles are not already in place at your church. I have not encountered many churches (zero would be precise) that have them perfected. You are not alone—not by a long shot. Just like any vision for the future, it is out there, and we are still here. The only way to get to that future is to start on the journey today knowing where we intend to end up.

There is good news! Simply choose to make these guiding principles your own. Instantly you will be on the path that makes these principles a reality in your leadership and in your church culture. When you embrace these beliefs as your desired truth, something miraculous happens. You will immediately begin to see opportunities to refine what you are doing right now to move closer to that truth.

---

[53] Ephesians 4:32
[54] Colossians 3:23-24 and Hebrews 12:1-3

SECRET #8: *Lead with Humility—Listen More, Talk Less*

For example, if you say it is easy to get connected to serve at your church, you will see places where you can expand your serving opportunities to make it true. Or perhaps clarify your screening processes to make it easier to get the right person in the right job. Or improve your promotional activities to inform people where their talents can be used. Once the principle is clear in your mind, and you are committed to it, your path becomes clearer as well. If you don't know where you are going, "then it doesn't matter which way you go."[55] Principles guide us where we desire to go.

LISTEN MORE TO YOUR VOLUNTEERS – PART ONE – MINISTRY FEEDBACK

Listen more to your Volunteers by asking for regular feedback on ministry efforts—especially those core activities that are cyclical or frequently repeated. Volunteers on the front lines are doing the work. They may have great ideas for streamlining processes or increasing effectiveness. Ask them. The truth is—we need to raise the bar—which should not come as a surprise to anyone. Just start with the assumption: If it is run by human beings, it could use some improving—this side of heaven. This is also a good personal philosophy for all of us who want to do the very best job we can. After all, God gave us His very best. Is it a leap of faith to infer that He would like our best efforts as well? Hence the guiding principle: "Excellence in everything we do honors God and inspires people."

By analyzing our results, we can determine if we have actually achieved our expected outcomes. We will know how to tweak future projects to make them even better. Do you just want success? Or SUCCESS? Or OUTRAGEOUS SUCCESS? How can OUTRAGEOUS SUCCESS happen if we do not know what

---

[55] Cheshire Cat from Lewis Carroll's 1865 *Alice's Adventures in Wonderland*.

worked and what did not? Who better to include in that assessment than the folks who were there on the front lines?

Remember from **SECRET #6:** ***Tap into Built-In Enthusiasm*** two of the three universal encouragers are being <u>part of something bigger than self</u> and to <u>making a positive difference</u>. As a leader, if you create opportunities for people to be part of BHAGs ("Big, Hairy, Audacious Goals")[56], they will flock to you.

Evaluating real outcomes against desired outcomes does not have to be scary or make us feel like failures. God already knows our shortcomings as well as our potential. Do we have any idea what we might have achieved? Probably not. All we really know for sure is that we got some results. To grow that "some" into "maximum," ask a couple of key questions after any event:

1. **What worked well? How do we know?**
2. **What did not work as well as we hoped? How do we know that?**
3. **What could we do differently the next time to get closer to what God had in mind?**

No blame necessary. We are just Monday-morning quarterbacking. We have next week's game to think about. What did we do well? What could we do better next time? No guilt. No shame.

If you get in the habit of doing a regular **W2 (What Worked) Assessment,** you will be increasing your leadership effectiveness in two ways. First, you will discover new ways to improve what you are doing—no small accomplishment. Second, your Volunteers will view you as a wonderful leader since you have shown the good sense to seek and value their opinions about the

---

[56] BHAGs ("Big, Hairy, Audacious Goals"), term made popular from *Built to Last: Successful Habits of Visionary Companies*; Jim Collins and Jerry Porras, 1994.

SECRET #8: *Lead with Humility—Listen More, Talk Less*

work they do. Make it a point to seek input from your Volunteers as a group – annually or pre/post major projects. See **APPENDIX 8A:** *W2 Assessment Worksheet* to help you get started.

Implementing a formal plan to seek input from Volunteers minimizes the awkwardness created by the unsolicited, isolated, not-so-well-thought-out suggestion. You are seeking collective wisdom and have put a system in place to acquire it. Then as the leader, of course, you add your own additional insights and judgment to decide what changes make the most sense. Please note: You are not turning your ministry into majority rule. You are not falling prey to becoming a *wishy-washy people pleaser*. You are still laser-focused on the one you want to please—God. You are seeking excellence which "honors God and inspires people." (See how those guiding principles help us stay focused on the prize?)

Conducting **What Worked Sessions (W2's)** following major events or projects is a great way to show Volunteers that they are important to you and that they are major contributors to the ministry's success. This also reinforces one of the strongest Volunteer motivators: Volunteers want to make a positive difference! Great leaders help Volunteers recognize the positive impact they have made.

LISTEN MORE TO YOUR VOLUNTEERS – PART TWO – LEADERSHIP FEEDBACK

Listen more to your Volunteers by asking for regular feedback on your leadership effectiveness. "It is much more difficult to judge oneself than to judge others. If you succeed in judging yourself rightly, then you are indeed a man of true wisdom."[57]

I think the Bible said it even better, "Why do you look at the

---

[57] Antoine de Saint Exupéry, French writer, in *The Little Prince*, 1943, in section 10. (Originally published in *Le Petit Prince* as "Il est bien plus difficile de se juger soi-même que de juger autrur. Si tu réussis à bien te juger, c'est que tu es un véritable sage.")

speck of sawdust in your brother's eye and pay no attention to the plank in your own eye?"[58] Do not be embarrassed, we are just being human. If you adopt the mindset to become a never-ending *work-in-progress*, there is no limit to how great a leader you can become.

It may seem counterintuitive to be transparent and let your staff/Volunteers know that you are less than perfect. ("Won't they think less of me?") No, they already know you are not perfect. Besides, they will be relieved. It is tough hanging around *Mr. Perfect* and *Ms. Amazing* 24/7. You will set a wonderful standard for everyone if you take seriously your role as a *work-in-progress*. You are letting them know that you are dead serious about wanting to fulfill God's expectations for you, and you need their help to do it. Remember the plank in the eye thing? You also become a positive role model for how to receive compassionate criticism. (See **SECRET #3:** *Compassionate Criticism.*) As a leader, no doubt you will be giving constructive feedback to them at some point. Wouldn't it be nice if they received it as well as you did? Be a role model for how to do it well.

If you are ready to venture into the land of self-improvement, you will find **APPENDIX 8B:** *Leadership Self-Assessment* to be a helpful tool. It includes sixteen specific leadership skills in four key areas. Each of the sixteen was rated as either 1st or 2nd in importance by individuals in test groups of life-long ministry Volunteers. What this tells us is that every one of these skills is valued highly by Volunteers who commit their lives to service—the kind of Volunteers you want to keep. If you are interested in knowing how these Volunteers have described great leaders, check it out.

The first step is to candidly evaluate your leadership behavior. The data shows where you think you are excelling and where you

---

[58] Matthew 7:3, NIV

SECRET #8: *Lead with Humility—Listen More, Talk Less*

need to step it up—by your own assessment. No one else has to be involved—just you. (This can't be that scary.) Simply start with the lowest scores. Even if you choose not to seek feedback from others, you will still have a clearer idea of what to improve. See **APPENDIX 8C:** *Directions for Analyzing Leadership Self-Assessment* to help you to glean the most value from your personal data.

Step two (a slightly braver move) is to ask for your team's assessment. See **APPENDIX 8D:** *Team Member Survey.* To get the most candid and honest feedback, I recommend asking that the feedback be given anonymously. Ask or assign one Volunteer to collect the data and tabulate the averages for you. After receiving that data, you may be surprised to find they have rated you higher in some areas than you have rated yourself. You may also discover areas where you thought you were successfully connecting only to find out you have not been as successful as you had hoped. This is a blessing in disguise—a rare opportunity to understand your team better and what they need from you to support their success. Remember, they want to be everything that God intended for them to be as well. This really can be a win-win.

LISTEN MORE TO YOUR VOLUNTEERS – PART THREE – REAL FEEDBACK FROM REAL VOLUNTEERS

Over the last seven years as I have been writing this book, I have had the privilege of talking with hundreds of Christian Volunteers—life-long, involved, high-impact Volunteers. I wanted to hear straight from the horse's mouth what they really thought about their leaders. And guess what? For the most part, they love you to pieces—warts and all. They love you because you give them the opportunity to serve God, to make a difference for someone or to be a small part of what a Big God is doing in the world. They know that one can serve God anywhere, but you create a time and place and clarity of purpose. It is concrete. What a gift! I hope you can appreciate how much they appreciate you. That, by the way, does not mean that you do not drive them crazy at times.

I specifically asked them about the unique qualities of great leaders and what advice they might have for the leader who wanted to go from "Good to Great."[59] The fact that you are reading this book and trying to improve your strategies tells me you are a good leader. Poor leaders seem happily oblivious to their negative impact on Volunteers. If they think anything at all about improvement, it is most likely "where can I find *new and improved* Volunteers?" You, however, want to be the best that God intended. Enjoy and be blessed by the advice that follows from real-life Volunteers to real-life leaders.

TOP 10 VOLUNTEER RECOMMENDATIONS FOR GREAT LEADERS

1. "Delegate – don't abdicate. We still need you to check back to see if we need anything or if we are on track. Fake-delegating drives us crazy too (i.e., giving us a task then completely re-doing it yourself without giving us a chance to correct our mistakes)."

2. "Be trustworthy and willing to trust us. You don't have to micro-manage."

3. "Be predictable. If you are consistent in your behavior, we can figure out a way to work with you and get the job done. It is very difficult when we don't know who is going to show up."

4. "Great leaders aren't afraid to raise up new leaders. Give

---

[59] Jim Collins, *Good to Great: Why Some Companies Make the Leap...and Others Don't*. One of the basic premises of this secular leadership book is that the biggest obstacle to GREAT is GOOD. GOOD too often becomes *good enough* even when GREAT is achievable.

SECRET #8: *Lead with Humility—Listen More, Talk Less*

us opportunities to learn leadership skills."

5. "Keep the vision in front of us to help us know we are making a Kingdom Impact. Sometimes it is too easy to get caught up in the job. Call our attention to the 'God moments' in our area of ministry."

6. "Please control the quality of the Volunteers. Some people volunteer but don't have the time to do a good job. Poor quality drags everybody down."
(Remember the guiding principle: "Excellence honors God and inspires people." The opposite is also true.)

7. "Encourage development of new skills or learning new things. Don't leave us stuck in the same place forever."

8. "CREATE a DEADLINE for GREAT IDEAS – rather than constantly changing things right up to *Go-Time*. Arbitrarily changing plans at the last minute is highly stressful" (a.k.a., GICO).[60]

9. "Try to keep your Volunteers working in their area of giftedness or passion." (Or at least target the Pareto 80/20 Rule: 80% of the time in area of giftedness/20% of the time doing the grunt work that accompanies every task.)

10. Check out the 16 skills identified in **APPENDIX 8B: *Ministry Leadership Self-Assessment*.** These are the essential day-to-day behaviors that Volunteers want and need.

---

[60] GICO, military term for **Great Idea Cut Off**

TOP 10 REASONS WHY VOLUNTEERS QUIT
or WILL NOT START IN THE FIRST PLACE

1. I am afraid of being stuck in the job till the *Second Coming*!

2. I feel unappreciated or unnoticed for my time and effort.

3. It's a Bad Talent Fit (example: I am an Introverted or shy person and you are trying to guilt me into being a Greeter).

4. Piling on work because you know it is difficult for me to say "No."

5. Using GUILT as a motivation.

6. I perceive my task as unimportant or unnecessary. "If it doesn't get done, that's okay" (i.e., Kingdom Impact is missing).

7. I have been previously caught in a *Bait & Switch* by another leader: "This will only take you 1-hour per week." How do I know you are describing this job accurately?

8. There is a personality *oil & water* conflict with the Ministry Leader or another Volunteer. Or there is a church conflict with another family member—"Love me, love my family."

9. Fear of failure (i.e., no training, mentoring or support provided).

10. "Your meetings drive me crazy—always run over-time. I don't feel like you respect my time or availability."

SECRET #8: *Lead with Humility—Listen More, Talk Less*

You have just heard from real Volunteers about what it takes to GROW from GOOD to GREAT. You have the tools to help you. All that is left is the desire and the commitment to be the best leader that God intends you to be. Go for it! You have what it takes!

Please think about letting someone know how you are doing and what creative things you are implementing to achieve your goals. Maybe others can learn from what you are doing to move towards 100% participation. Please see **SECRET 8½: *Strategically PLAN to Succeed*** to learn the half-secret that will help you to reach your goals.

☑ Action Steps to Improve My Leadership:

☐ 1. Create some BHAGs ("Big, Hairy, Audacious Goals")[61] to inspire people.
According to God and human creativity guru Walt Disney, "It's kind of fun to do the impossible."[62]

☐ 2. Evaluate one ministry project or on-going process. See **APPENDIX 8A:** *W2 Analysis* **WORKSHEET.**

☐ 3. Assess your leadership strengths by taking the *Leadership Self-Assessment.* See **APPENDICES 8B** and **8C.**

☐ 4. Be gutsy. Ask for team feedback. See **APPENDIX 8D:** *Team Member Survey.*

☐ 5. Go to www.JuneKenny.com for free training Worksheets, helpful tips on working with Volunteers, to participate in discussions and to share your ideas.

Leadership Makes a Difference

"If your actions inspire others to dream more, learn more, do more and become more, you are a leader."
– John Quincy Adams
6th President of the United States

---

[61] BHAGs ("Big, Hairy, Audacious Goals").
[62] Walt Disney (American motion-picture Producer, pioneer of animated cartoon films. 1901-1966).

SECRET #8: *Lead with Humility—Listen More, Talk Less*

☑ Actions I Plan to Take to Improve My Leadership:

1. _____

2. _____

3. _____

4. _____

5. _____

6. _____

7. _____

8. _____

APPENDIX 8A: *W2 (What Worked) Analysis* WORKSHEET p.1 of 2

Our ACTIVITY /PROCEDURE /PROJECT:

_____

STEP ONE: Identify the important *parts or stages* of the activity, procedure or project to be analyzed. (Examples: planning, publicity/promotion, registration, set-up, decoration, clean-up, program, speakers, childcare, transportation, hospitality, food preparation, teamwork, etc.) Review the parts independently.

Analysis of (*part/stage*):_____

QUESTIONS TO ASK:

1. *(W2)* What worked well?

2. How do we know that?

3. *(W2)* What did not work as well as we hoped?

4. How do we know that?

APPENDIX 8A: *W2 (What Worked) Analysis* WORKSHEET p.2 of 2

5. What could we do differently next time to get closer to what God had in mind?

   ☐

   ☐

   ☐

   ☐

   ☐

   ☐

   ☐

6. Who will be responsible to make this happen? ...or to remind us?

   Name: _____

   Phone: _____

   Email: _____

APPENDIX 8B: *Leadership Self-Assessment* p.1 of 3

Enhancing Your Leadership Skills:
Going from GOOD to GREAT

Great leadership achieves greater success through people. To excel, it helps to know our strengths as well as those specific areas we need to improve. This assessment is designed to help Ministry Leaders better understand how their leadership skills are perceived by others.

Instructions: On a scale of 1 (Never) to 10 (Always), please indicate how **others would describe** your current leadership style. Circle the number that best represents their response to each of the following statements. **Circle only one number for each statement.**
Note: This is for *"your eyes only"* so please **be totally honest with yourself**.

Self-Perception Survey

Based on my past experience interacting with others, I believe **others would rate me as follows**:

▽ TEAM AVG.   ▽ GAP

                      Never   **Always**

1. Treats team members Professionally and with respect at all times.   1 2 3 4 5 6 7 8 9 10   ____ ____

2. Supports team members' success by providing appropriate training and resource support when needed.   1 2 3 4 5 6 7 8 9 10   ____ ____

APPENDIX 8B: *Leadership Self-Assessment* p.2 of 3

	Never Always	TEAM AVG.	GAP

3. Shows team members that they are important as individuals apart from the work they do.   1 2 3 4 5 6 7 8 9 10   ____   ____

4. Encourages and supports the on-going spiritual development of team members.   1 2 3 4 5 6 7 8 9 10   ____   ____

5. Communicates work expectations clearly and with enough detail to be successful.   1 2 3 4 5 6 7 8 9 10   ____   ____

6. <u>Listens</u> when there are ideas on how to do things better.   1 2 3 4 5 6 7 8 9 10   ____   ____

7. Handles *giving* correction with grace, dignity and respect (i.e., "Compassionate Criticism").   1 2 3 4 5 6 7 8 9 10   ____   ____

8. <u>Asks</u> for others' ideas or input.   1 2 3 4 5 6 7 8 9 10   ____   ____

9. Shows appreciation for good work both formally and informally.   1 2 3 4 5 6 7 8 9 10   ____   ____

APPENDIX 8B: *Leadership Self-Assessment* p.3 of 3

	Never Always	TEAM AVG.	GAP
10. Plans and facilitates meetings that result in clear outcomes or achieve the stated goals. Respects everyone's time.	1 2 3 4 5 6 7 8 9 10	_____	_____
11. Well-organized: plans ahead; sets goals & priorities; then takes appropriate action to complete them.	1 2 3 4 5 6 7 8 9 10	_____	_____
12. Handles **CONFLICT** calmly and respectfully in a straight-forward and timely manner.	1 2 3 4 5 6 7 8 9 10	_____	_____
13. Reliable, consistent, follows through on his/her commitments in a timely manner.	1 2 3 4 5 6 7 8 9 10	_____	_____
14. Handles *receiving* criticism with grace, dignity and respect (i.e., maturity, self-control, openness).	1 2 3 4 5 6 7 8 9 10	_____	_____
15. Keeps others informed of status (verbally or in writing) on things that affect them.	1 2 3 4 5 6 7 8 9 10	_____	_____
16. Generously shares the credit/praise with the team.	1 2 3 4 5 6 7 8 9 10	_____	_____

APPENDIX 8C: *Directions for Analyzing Leadership Self-Assessment*

Enhancing Your Ministry Leadership:
Going from GOOD to GREAT

Directions for Analyzing your Self-Perception Survey & Team Member Feedback

Congratulations!

You have just taken a major step toward becoming the GREAT leader God intends you to be. You have carefully and honestly evaluated your current leadership practices. By your own assessment, you have rated yourself higher in some areas and lower in others.

Growth and improvement occur when we focus on clear, behavior-focused targets. It is not enough to *want to be a better leader*. It requires doing the things that GREAT LEADERS do to achieve the results that they do.

Please note: Each of these 16 skills was rated as either 1st or 2nd in Importance by individuals in test groups of high-impact ministry Volunteers. What this tells us is that **every one of these skills is valued highly** by those Volunteers who commit their lives to service—the kind of Volunteers you want to keep.

STEP ONE: Identify the THREE SKILLS (#1-16) that you have rated yourself the lowest.

ASK: "What specific behaviors can I practice to improve…?"

197

APPENDIX 8C: *Directions for Analyzing Leadership Self-Assessment*

LOW SCORES:

#1 _____
　　　(skill)

_____

_____

_____

#2 _____
　　　(skill)

_____

_____

_____

#3 _____
　　　(skill)

_____

_____

_____

Make a **30-day Commitment** to practice your identified behaviors. You will be surprised how quickly they will become *second nature* to you. Once they do, tackle the additional skills you want to add or improve.

APPENDIX 8C: *Directions for Analyzing Leadership Self-Assessment*

STEP TWO: Identify a **SPECIFIC AREA** to Target for Growth

Record your Self-Assessment SCORES in the following categories: **T / C / P & O / S-M**

Questions:

TEAMWORK

1 _____
2 _____
3 _____
4 _____

TOTAL = _____ ÷ 4 = _____
                                                (AVG.)

COMMUNICATION

5 _____
6 _____
7 _____
8 _____
9 _____

TOTAL = _____ ÷ 5 = _____
                                                (AVG.)

APPENDIX 8C: *Directions for Analyzing Leadership Self-Assessment*

PLANNING / ORGANIZATION

\# 10 _____

\# 11 _____

TOTAL = _____ ÷ 2 = _____

(AVG.)

SELF-MANAGEMENT

\# 12 _____

\# 13 _____

\# 14 _____

\# 15 _____

\# 16 _____

TOTAL = _____ ÷ 5 = _____

(AVG.)

ASK YOURSELF: In what area do I show the greatest strength right now?

T / C / P & O / S-M

_____

What **_SPECIFIC AREA_** needs the most improvement right now? What specific behaviors can I implement to improve…?

_____
AREA TO IMPROVE

_____

_____

_____

APPENDIX 8C: *Directions for Analyzing Leadership Self-Assessment*

STEP THREE: Obtain Team Feedback

If you haven't already done so, tell your team about your sincere desire to be the best leader possible and ask for their candid feedback. Ask (or assign) one of them to serve as the *point person* who will collect the confidential surveys and calculate the average scores for you. You will receive only the averages for each of the 16 skill statements. Their feedback will help you assess your current skills from their perspective in the FOUR leadership areas. Be sure to thank them in advance for their support.

Once you receive your TEAM SCORES:
1. Circle the team score on your self-assessment using a different colored pen or marker. This will help you see where your assessment and your team's differ.
2. Write the **TEAM AVERAGE** in the space provided on the right.
3. Then, calculate and record your GAP SCORE in the space provided.

    The **GAP SCORE** is the difference between your "guess" and their "real life experience with you."

Possible results:

__0__ = (Both scores are the same)

+____ = (Their score is HIGHER than yours.) ☺

−____ = (Their score is LOWER than yours.) ☹

If the **GAP SCORE** is 2 or more points (+ or -), you have misunderstood your team's perception. *Out of touch* is not the most effective *location* from which to lead. A positive GAP SCORE, however, is always a pleasant surprise! It means that you are more effective in that area

APPENDIX 8C: *Directions for Analyzing Leadership Self-Assessment*

than you thought. ☺ A negative GAP SCORE is not the end of the world. Please remember that Volunteers are not looking for perfection. They just want someone who wants to do great things, wants to include them, and embraces a little humility. Sincerely asking them to help you become what God intended will honor them and buy you a lot of forgiveness for future mistakes. Not a bad bargain.

4. Identify any skills where your **GAP SCORE** is –2 points or more.
   This can be great discussion starter with your team.
   "I was lower on that skill than I thought. What kinds of things could I be doing differently to better meet your needs in that area?"

   If the corrective behavior is obvious to all or cooperative in nature –
   "Thank you for your feedback. You are right. Our meetings could be more focused and productive. Let's see what we could do together to make sure our meetings are effective and end on time. What suggestions do you have?"
   Own up to the problem. Express your enthusiasm for fixing it. Involve them in the solution.

5. Plan to have a candid discussion about what you have learned from your assessment with your team, mentors, or other leaders you respect (or all three!) to discuss strategies for your continued growth into the leader both you and God want.

APPENDIX 8C: *Directions for Analyzing Leadership Self-Assessment*

IDEAS:

SKILL TO IMPROVE

_____
_____
_____

SKILL TO IMPROVE

_____
_____
_____

APPENDIX 8D: *Team Member Survey* p.1 of 3

Helping Ministry Leaders go from GOOD to GREAT

Team Member Survey

To my team members:
It is my desire to be the best Ministry Leader that God intended. To achieve this life-long goal, your honest and thoughtful feedback is important and deeply appreciated. Thank you in advance for your time and your wisdom.

Instructions: On a scale of 1 (Never) to 10 (Always), please indicate how you would describe **my current leadership style**. Circle the number that best represents your response to each of the following statements.

Circle only one number for each statement.

Note: All response sheets are anonymous and will remain confidential.

Please return this sheet to _____ who will tabulate the average score for each of the 16 leadership skills and present the TEAM AVERAGES to me.

Thank you!

                                                                                Never   **Always**

1. Treats team members professionally and with respect at all times.   1 2 3 4 5 6 7 8 9 10

2. Supports team members' success by providing appropriate training and resource support when needed.   1 2 3 4 5 6 7 8 9 10

3. Shows team members that they are important as individuals apart from the work they do.   1 2 3 4 5 6 7 8 9 10

APPENDIX 8D: *Team Member Survey* p.2 of 3

		Never **Always**
4.	Encourages and supports the on-going spiritual development of team members.	1 2 3 4 5 6 7 8 9 10
5.	Communicates work expectations clearly and with enough detail to be successful.	1 2 3 4 5 6 7 8 9 10
6.	<u>Listens</u> when there are ideas on how to do things better.	1 2 3 4 5 6 7 8 9 10
7.	Handles *giving* correction with grace, dignity and respect (i.e., "Compassionate Criticism").	1 2 3 4 5 6 7 8 9 10
8.	<u>Asks</u> for others' ideas or input.	1 2 3 4 5 6 7 8 9 10
9.	Shows appreciation for good work both formally and informally.	1 2 3 4 5 6 7 8 9 10
10.	Plans and facilitates meetings that result in clear outcomes or achieve the stated goals. Respects everyone's time.	1 2 3 4 5 6 7 8 9 10
11.	Well-organized: plans ahead; sets goals & priorities; then takes appropriate action to complete them.	1 2 3 4 5 6 7 8 9 10
12.	Handles **CONFLICT** calmly and respectfully in a straight-forward and timely manner.	1 2 3 4 5 6 7 8 9 10
13.	Reliable, consistent, follows through on his/her commitments in a timely manner.	1 2 3 4 5 6 7 8 9 10

APPENDIX 8D: *Team Member Survey* p.3 of 3

		Never **Always**
14.	Handles *receiving* criticism with grace, dignity and respect (i.e., maturity, self-control, openness).	1 2 3 4 5 6 7 8 9 10
15.	Keeps others informed of status (verbally or in writing) on things that affect them.	1 2 3 4 5 6 7 8 9 10
16.	Generously shares the credit/praise with the team.	1 2 3 4 5 6 7 8 9 10

#8½: Part A—
Strategically PLAN to Succeed!
Part B—
Plan *in advance* to Share your Success!

So, how do we do that?

Planning. We Christians are painfully aware that our human plans are written in the sand, ever subject to changes imposed by the world or improved by God's handiwork. Since they are so likely to be changed or even scrapped, how important is planning?

God endorses planning. In fact, He is the Great Planner. Be awed by His universe. Be amazed by the complexity of the world and its interconnected, interdependent systems. Is there really any question about intelligent design? Do you truly believe God was winging it? Not likely. "Planning is bringing the future into the present so that you can do something about it now."[63]

Find out what God wants you to do, and plan how to do the best job you possibly can. According to Stephen Covey, "If you clearly understand where you want to be, you can make sure that your actions bring you closer to that place each and every day."[64] If it is your desire to succeed with your ministry goal—and I am sure it is—develop a very specific plan to get there. Even better, write it down. Written goals are committed goals—committed in black and white. Written goals help you remember what you meant to do and, more importantly, they will help others understand how they can help you. When your plan exists only in your head, your great idea is a little foggy for the rest of us to see.

Plan *in advance* to Share your Success. An unexpected but

---

[63] Alan Lakein, author of *How to Get Control of Your Time and Your Life*.
[64] Stephen Covey, author of *7 Habits of Highly Effective People*.

important part of reaching a great goal is planning, up-front, to share that success with someone—anyone. For example, have you ever attended a conference or meeting knowing that you were expected to report back to those who could not attend? I will bet you took better notes, paid more attention and as a result absorbed more. That was no accident. Your future *intention* increased your current *attention* to learn more. The same phenomenon occurs when you plan to share your expected success. You will plan more carefully. You will track the progress and outcomes more carefully. This up-front goal setting, along with your intention to share, will be invaluable to you when you assess what worked, what did not and what you can do better the next time. It will also be invaluable to others who might want to learn from you—without having to reinvent the wheel or fall in the same potholes.

We can achieve greater results by learning from each other. **Plan *in advance* to Share Your Success. Be a Blessing to Others**! It is a Win-Win.

HALF-SECRET

Unlike the previous secrets, this secret is not complete. You will need to supply the second half to make it work. **Strategically PLAN to Succeed**—you must decide what to plan. **Plan *in advance* to Share Your Success**—you must decide with whom to do that. Perhaps you have a sister church, neighboring church or similarly-situated church with whom to share ideas and solutions to common challenges.

The important thing is that you know you will be responsible for explaining what you did and how it turned out—warts and all. Remember, we are all works in progress! Your up-front goal to be a blessing to others will also actively contribute to your success.

POSSIBLE OPPORTUNITIES TO CONSIDER FOR GROWTH and DEVELOPMENT

(APPENDIX 8½A: *Discussion Handout*)

- ☑ Promoting and Publicizing Volunteer Opportunities

- ☑ Expanding Volunteer Opportunities

- ☑ Making it Easier to Get Connected at _____
  your church name

- ☑ Making it Easier to Serve at _____
  your church name

- ☑ Effective Screening Processes

- ☑ Matching Volunteers to the Right Volunteer Opportunity

- ☑ Training and Equipping Volunteers to Succeed

- ☑ Leadership Development (for both Volunteers and Staff) (Mentoring, Shepherding, Coaching and Supervising Skills)

- ☑ Identifying Future Leaders

- ☑ On-going Care and Feeding of Volunteers

- ☑ Volunteer Appreciation Strategies

- ☑ Developing a Church-wide Volunteer Support System

- ☑ Or? ___(insert your idea here)_____

Could your church or Christian organization benefit from improving any of the above categories? Excellent! There are exciting opportunities ahead to be more of what God intended! The next section will help you organize your thoughts in ways that achieve successful outcomes.

> *"You can't get to where you're going if you don't know where where is."*[65]

PLAN YOUR SUCCESS BY CREATING SMART GOALS[66]

Now that you have some areas in mind where you might be open to creating some new goals for your ministry, take a look at what goes into a great goal. Great goals are **S.M.A.R.T.** — **Specific, Measurable, Achievable, Relevant** and **Time-Bound**.

S.M.A.R.T. GOALS ARE SPECIFIC—
The What & The Why

The What & The Why are two types of goals that identify what we are going to do immediately (the **"What-Goal"**) and why we are doing it (the **"Why-Goal"**). One is an immediate action—easy to get our brains around. The second, and clearly most important, is our hoped for Kingdom impact—the real reason for doing anything at all. What exactly are we hoping to positively impact by taking some immediate action? Usually this is a bigger, longer-term, more significant, God-sized challenge: get more folks *off the bench* and *into the game*, expand Christian education to reach more children, deepen spiritual development, build closer Christian community, etc.

Too often I have seen Ministry Leaders focus exclusively on the **"What-Goal"**: an appreciation dinner, pins for Volunteer

---

[65] Anonymous but very wise person.
[66] Doran, G. T. (1981). "There's a S.M.A.R.T. way to write management's goals and objectives." Management Review (AMA FORUM) 70 (11): 35–36.

SECRET #8½: *Strategically PLAN to Succeed!*

service, a recognition program, etc. without much consideration of the **"Why-Goal"**. In fact, churches typically do a great job with the details of a **"What-Goal"**. However, the more important question to consider up-front is "Why are we having a dinner, pins, program, etc.?" What do we hope to achieve long-term by doing them? Do these specific actions (the **"What-Goals"**) successfully achieve our **"Why-Goal"**?

Please note: rarely does a specific action have inherent success value. Pins do not automatically motivate or make Volunteers feel appreciated. In fact, truth be known, pins can de-motivate, especially when tracking of Volunteer service is sloppy. Food, however tasty, does not automatically make a Volunteer feel valued. When we want to show appreciation, honor or motivate Volunteers (a **"Why-Goal"**), we need to choose the best **"What-Goal"** that will get us where we want to go.

Let's look first at how to create a crystal clear, very specific **"Why-Goal"**. A poor example would be "We want more Volunteer Participation." What is wrong with this? It sounds important enough. The problem is it's too vague. A better example might be "Our Goal is 100% Participation." One hundred percent *off the bench* and *into the game* might scare a few ministry folks, but this kind of **BHAG** ("Big, Hairy, Audacious Goal")[67] could mobilize your entire church, every ministry, everybody and everything. There are plenty of Biblical references to persuade us that God intends all of us to be involved.[68] And, most assuredly, there is plenty of work to be done.[69] The point is: if we hope to mobilize the energy of potential Volunteers, we need to make sure our goals are laser-focused and big enough to inspire.

What if we said we wanted to increase Volunteer participation by 50%? Would that be clear enough for us to identify the best

---

[67] BHAG ("Big, Hairy, Audacious Goal").
[68] John 13:12-17; Galatians 5:13; Philippians 2:3-4; Galatians 6:10
[69] Ephesians 2:10

possible **"What-Goal"**? Again, probably not. Here is why. As it is currently stated, this **"Why-Goal"** could be interpreted to mean two different things, each requiring a different strategy for the **"What-Goal"**. For example, if you currently have 100 Volunteers, are you saying you want to have 150 by a specific date? If so, your strategy will be focused on recruitment of new Volunteers. On the other hand, perhaps you want your current Volunteers to become more committed and deepen their involvement by 50%. If each one currently serves 2 hours per month (24 hours per year), your target goal might be 3 hours per month (36 hours per year). The best strategy for this would be to focus on Volunteer encouragement, increasing responsibilities of jobs, leadership development, etc. Maybe you want both? One hundred Volunteers at 2 hours per month is 2,400 labor-hours per year, but 150 Volunteers at 3 hours per month is a whopping 5,400 hours! What could you do in your ministry with that?

The bottom line is this: the best strategy to achieve the first goal was not the best strategy to achieve the second. Until you have clearly defined the bigger target you are hoping to positively impact (your **"Why-Goal"**), you will not know how to effectively direct your efforts. It is said that the *devil is in the details*. I say *God* is all about details. When He counts the hairs on your head,[70] He values details. I think the devil does his best to keep our thinking foggy because he is afraid of what we might achieve if we got our act together. Think **SPECIFICS**—1ˢᵗ the **"Why"**, and then, 2ⁿᵈ the **"What"**.

S.M.A.R.T. GOALS ARE <u>MEASURABLE</u>

How will we know if we have achieved our goal? What will we likely see if we are successful? It depends, doesn't it? If we are looking for increased hours of service per Volunteer, we can count

---

[70] Matthew 10:30; Luke 12:4-7

(or estimate) the hours given. See **SECRET #1**'s **APPENDIX 1B: *Calculate Ministry Labor Hours*** for how-to tips. If we are looking for increased total number of people, we can count the people. The key question: "What are we looking for to show us that our arrow hit the target?" Maybe the measurement is simply "Did we do it?" If the goal was to read a book on leading Volunteers, and you read this one, you did it. Goal achieved. But unless what you read translates into some positive leadership behavior that successfully impacts Volunteer service, it will not meet the **RELEVANT** criterion below. "The greatest danger for most of us lies not in setting our aim too high and falling short; but in setting our aim too low, and achieving our mark."[71]

S.M.A.R.T. GOALS ARE <u>ATTAINABLE</u>

Our goal must be **ATTAINABLE** with the time, talent and resources we have at hand or can muster. For example, simply saying we want everyone in the congregation to be engaged in service may be more of a wish (right now) than an actionable undertaking. Without the volunteer support system in place to manage the volume of Volunteers, it would be impossible.

One of my pet peeves is the annual unilateral appeal for people to volunteer when no real support plan has been put in place to sort the multitude of slips of paper dropped in the collection plate. When potential Volunteers respond, and no one calls them back, they may not bother the next time. Trust me here, it has happened. Kudos to you if your church is exempt from this all too common faux pas.

Once you have determined where you want to go, think clearly through your plans to successfully get there. You do not want to have to downsize your plan in the middle, end up with a mediocre

---

[71] Michelangelo Buonarroti, Italian sculptor, painter, architect, engineer (1475-1564).

outcome or burn out your Volunteers in the attempt. Perhaps you will uncover some missing pieces that need to be in place before this particular goal is attempted. This can be a good thing. Ensuring your success up front by thoughtful, realistic planning makes it a lot easier not only to marshal support for the current project but will also get Volunteers to follow you the next time. You develop the reputation as a leader who knows what they are doing and knows how to succeed. Please note: this is not an admonition to think small. By all means THINK BIG! You are working for a BIG GOD who has BIG PLANS for you. Volunteers want to make a difference (see **SECRET #6: *Tap into Built-In Enthusiasm*)** by working with leaders who know how to do that.

...thoughtful, realistic planning makes it a lot easier not only to marshal support for the current project but will also get Volunteers to follow you the next time.

S.M.A.R.T. GOALS ARE RELEVANT

Our goal must be **RELEVANT** to our organization's vision and our targeted Kingdom Impact—the **"Why-Goal"**. In truth, **RELEVANT** ought to be listed as the first requirement of any SMART GOAL. If it were though, we would not have the helpful acronym SMART to help us remember how to create successful goals. RATS-M just does not have the same sticking power. **RELEVANT** answers the question, "Will this dinner, background check, welcome letter, etc. help us get closer to our goal?" WHY and WHAT are not the same thing. A **"What-Goal"** is merely the immediate action we think or hope will achieve our true purpose—the **"Why-Goal"**. Since the terms "goal" and "purpose" are so

SECRET #8½: *Strategically PLAN to Succeed!*

often used interchangeably in conversation, it can be very confusing. It is helpful when we clarify our terminology to differentiate **"Why-Goals"** from **"What-Goals"**. Here is a real-life example to illustrate how easy it is to confuse the two.

Like many larger churches, this church of 2,000 attendees found they had an on-going challenge to create a sense of community and foster one-on-one relationships. The women's ministry was preparing for their Annual Women's Dinner. When I asked why they were going to have a dinner, their answer surprised me. In truth, I think my question surprised them. Their reply, "We always have one." Granted, I understand history and tradition, but why a dinner versus something else? No answer. "Why" is a simple but important question to ask. If we do not know why we are doing something, how will we ever know if our good efforts have made a positive impact somewhere? Do not get me wrong, there are lots of positive reasons for a church to have a special women's dinner.[72] The purpose you choose guides your planning of the event to ensure that your specific targeted purpose is achieved.

In the above example, the best I could discern from attending the women's dinner was that they were having a dinner to have a dinner. As a result, the planning seemed to be focused on food preparation and decorations. The food was delicious, of course. But was that all they wanted to happen? I am certain, somewhere deep down, they were hoping for more than successful caloric consumption.

Little publicity preceded the event. Attendance was poor. Perhaps they were marketing by way of the "Build It and They Will Come"[73] strategy. In church lingo, "God will make sure the

---

[72] Possible Goals for Women's Dinner include: facilitate personal connection, strengthen relationships, create a sense of belonging, spiritual development, global or local ministry awareness, Volunteer recruitment, leadership development, Volunteer appreciation, celebration, inspiration, team development, etc.

[73] 1989 Movie *Field of Dreams*

right people are here."[74] But maybe God wanted us to make the effort to ask a few more of our friends. Some of the prepared tables remained empty. Even though the main group participation activity had been carefully prepared, one table of ladies simply refused to participate. Why? They longed for relationship-building. They wanted to enjoy each other's company rather than play a contrived game that had no obvious connection to anything. Those of us who engaged in the prepared game found very little time for personal interaction. Perhaps the planners thought relationship-building would happen automatically. It does not. This was a meal. Period. I was not surprised that attendance had been dwindling over the years. Breaking bread together is not an end in itself. It is only a tool, an opportunity to…do what? If the planners had identified up-front that a specific purpose was to help women get to know each other better—a difficult task in a large congregation—the activity could have been designed to foster interaction. On the other hand, if the purpose had been to celebrate Women's Ministry, speakers could have shared heart-warming stories about the previous year's activities and successes. If the purpose had been to expand attendance in women's Bible study groups, upcoming exciting study opportunities could have been promoted. And so forth.

It is easy. First decide what big picture (Kingdom) challenge you want to positively impact. Then design the event, activity or process in a way that you think will best hit that target.

In the military, the Big Picture Goal (the **"Why-Goal"**) is known as *Commander's Intent (CI)*. Every soldier in the platoon is trained to know the *CI*. Even privates are free to alter their course of action, when necessary, to achieve that ultimate purpose. The point is that everyone knows what they are trying to achieve. Not "Capture Hill #39" (a **"What-Goal"**), but "Stop the Enemy" (the **"Why-Goal"**). Your Volunteers want to know your "CI". Knowing

---

[74] This is exactly the statement I had been given.

SECRET #8½: *Strategically PLAN to Succeed!*

your Kingdom purpose not only provides the clarity they need, it is motivating. (See **"Kingdom Impact"** in **SECRET #6: *Tap into Built-in Enthusiasm.*)** There is a lot to be said for spreading that information (i.e., motivation) around. How good is your organization at explaining the **"Why-Goal"** to your Volunteers?

Even if you are a newbie to leading, never fear asking "Why?" It can lead to clarity of purpose. Once we are clear about what we are attempting to do, we can get very creative about making it happen. Also never be afraid to ask, "How did we do?" How will we know if we hit the target? How will we hit the bulls-eye next time if we do not ask this time what worked and what did not? We have a responsibility to be good shepherds of the resources God has provided us. Maybe the finances could have or should have been spent in another way to achieve a greater outcome. Maybe the human effort could have or should have been used more wisely. Who better to ask than the Volunteers who were working on the front lines? Or the people who were served? See **SECRET #8: Lead with Humility—Listen More, Talk Less** for tips and tools to help you do this.

S.M.A.R.T. GOALS HAVE A TIME TARGET

Goals should have a **TIME TARGET.** This means set a date for expected successful completion. Often this is an obvious and specific date—the dinner is occurring on April 25th. Even when the end date is flexible, it is still an excellent idea to set a specific target date. This helps us to plan backward from end date to today. If we want to grow our Volunteer base from 100 to 150 in one year, we would expect to see some serious progress by the end of six months. If progress is not forthcoming, we have time to tweak our plan. An end-date creates a sense of urgency to stay focused on the goal and monitor progress.

UNEXPECTED BENEFITS

Ministry jobs are notorious for morphing into entirely different jobs. More often than not it results in expanding your responsibilities. New leaders may suddenly be on deck to carry out your former responsibilities. When clear goals (both the **"Why-Goal"** and the **"What-Goal"**) are described and written down, the next Ministry Leader does not have to start from square-one to figure out what is going on. They can look back to see what has been done before and what recommendations have been suggested to improve future efforts. No one has to re-invent the wheel. I don't know about you, but I would find that refreshing. I am just speculating, but it might even be easier to recruit Volunteers into leadership positions if some of this documentation existed to support them.

PLAN *in advance* TO SHARE YOUR SUCCESS!

You have carefully planned your success with every intention of sharing it with someone else. Kudos to you! As a result, your plans were clearly defined. Everyone knew what they were doing and why they were doing it. You tracked the progress and documented along the way. You noted the results at the end. You are ready. Who do you want to share with? Do you have an on-going ministry support group with your own denomination's local churches? Great! Or perhaps you have a cooperative relationship with other churches in your community? Would they be blessed by knowing how to do what you did? Or hearing your idea? If your project was creative or improved a Volunteer management problem, they probably would love to know. Also, conferences love new and creative "How To" breakout sessions. Why not offer your success idea to your regional conference planners?

Or better yet, share it with us. We would love to hear from you. When you go to our website, www.JuneKenny.com, you will find a link where you can tell us what you have done to improve

SECRET #8½: *Strategically PLAN to Succeed!*

Volunteer support in your church or Christian organization.

See **APPENDIX 8½B:** *Create SMART Goals* to help you plan. See **APPENDIX 8½C:** *Tracking Success Worksheet* to help you evaluate your outcomes. We will post the **"Best Ideas"** giving credit to your church or ministry group. This is a place where Volunteer leaders can go to get new ideas, ask questions, download free handouts, participate in discussion groups, brainstorm solutions and share their successes with other Christian organizations.

God blessed Abraham so that he would be a blessing to others.[75] God continually blesses us for the same reason—to be a blessing to others. Here is an opportunity for you to do just that. Be part of an ever-growing resource that will bless you while you bless others.

We are here to support you while you are supporting your Volunteers! We look forward to hearing from you.

---

[75] Genesis 12:2

☑ Action Steps to Increase Ministry Success:

☐ 1. Create **S.M.A.R.T. GOALS** for your next ministry project to get the hang of it. See **APPENDIX 8½B:** *Create S.M.A.R.T. Goals.*

☐ 2. Get input from your team to determine the best place to start. Use **APPENDIX 8½A:** *Discussion Handout* to prime the pump.

☐ 3. Go to www.JuneKenny.com for free training Worksheets, helpful tips on working with Volunteers and to participate in discussions.

☐ 4. Use **APPENDIX 8½C:** *Tracking Success Worksheet* to help you analyze your projects and determine what actions led to your success. Your future successes will be so much easier.

☐ 5. Go to www.JuneKenny.com to share your latest Volunteer success story. We would love to learn from you!

"We make a living by what we get,
but we make a life by what we give."
– Winston Churchill

SECRET #8½: *Strategically PLAN to Succeed!*

☑ Actions I Plan to Take to Increase My Ministry's Success:

1._____

2._____

3._____

4._____

5._____

6._____

7._____

8._____

APPENDIX 8½A: *Discussion Handout*

POSSIBLE OPPORTUNITIES TO CONSIDER FOR GROWTH and DEVELOPMENT

Could your church or Christian organization benefit from improving any of the following categories?

☐ Promoting and Publicizing Volunteer Opportunities

☐ Expanding Volunteer Opportunities

☐ Making it Easier to Get Connected at _____
   (your church name)

☐ Making it Easier to Serve at _____
   (your church name)

☐ Effective Screening Processes

☐ Matching Volunteers to the Right Volunteer Opportunity

☐ Training and Equipping Volunteers to Succeed

☐ Leadership Development (for both Volunteers and Staff) (Mentoring, Shepherding, Coaching and Supervising Skills)

☐ Identifying Future Leaders

☐ On-going Care and Feeding of Volunteers

☐ Volunteer Appreciation Strategies

☐ Developing a Church-wide Volunteer Support System

☐ *(insert your idea here)* _____

☐ _____

☐ _____

APPENDIX 8½B: *Create S.M.A.R.T. Goals*

Create S.M.A.R.T.[76] Goals

SPECIFIC:

1st Our **Why-Goal** is: _____
   (the big picture purpose – intended Kingdom Impact)

2nd Our **What-Goal** is: _____
   (the immediate action)
Details: who, what, when, where, how much, how many, etc.

MEASURABLE:

Observable results we will look for:

Our **Why-Goal**: _____

Our **What-Goal**: _____

We intend to measure our results by: _____

ACHIEVABLE:

What specific resources are needed for success:
   Expertise or Skills? Workers? Funding? Support? Time?

What resources do we have now?

What do we still need?

---

[76] Doran, G. T. (1981). "There's a S.M.A.R.T. way to write management's goals and objectives." Management Review (AMA FORUM) 70 (11): 35–36.

APPENDIX 8½B: *Create S.M.A.R.T. Goals*

Now that we have considered the costs in time, effort and money, how does this choice compare to our other choices?

RELEVANT:

In what way does this immediate action (the **What-Goal**) positively impact our Kingdom purpose?

How do we know?

Is this the **most relevant** immediate action we could choose at this time?

TIME-BOUND:

Our immediate action (the **What-Goal**) will be accomplished

by: _____.

We expect to see positive impact on our Kingdom purpose (the

Why-Goal) by: _____.

APPENDIX 8½C: *Tracking Success Worksheet* SUMMARY

Ministry: _____ **SUMMARY**
Date: _____ **TRACKING SUCCESS**
Ministry Leader: _____ **WORKSHEET**

DIRECTIONS:
Use the following worksheets to discuss what went well, what didn't and what you would do differently next time. Then, summarize your results on this page.

SUMMARY:

1st Our **Why-Goal** was: _____
   (the intended Kingdom impact)
   1. Did we have a + impact? How do we know?
   2. How would we rate our positive impact?

```
|---+---+---+---+---+---+---+---+---+---|
0   +1  +2  +3  +4  +5  +6  +7  +8  +9  +10
```

2nd Our **What-Goal** was: _____
   (the immediate action)
   After assessing each part of the activity, procedure or project, how do we rate our overall success?

```
|---+---+---+---+---+---+---+---+---+---|
0   +1  +2  +3  +4  +5  +6  +7  +8  +9  +10
```

APPENDIX 8½C: *Tracking Success Worksheet* SUMMARY

WHAT WENT WELL THIS TIME:

1.

2.

3.

4.

5.

IDEAS AND RECOMMENDATIONS FOR NEXT TIME ARE:

1.

2.

3.

4.

5.

6. Who will be responsible to make this happen? …or to remind us?

        Name: _____

        Phone: _____

        Email: _____

APPENDIX 8½C: *Tracking Success* WORKSHEET

Our **"What-Goal"** (activity, procedure, project, etc.) is:

_____

STEP ONE: Identify the important parts or stages of the activity, procedure or project to be analyzed. (Examples: planning, publicity/promotion, registration, set-up, decoration, clean-up, program, speakers, childcare, transportation, hospitality, food preparation, teamwork, etc.). Review the parts independently.

STEP TWO: Analyze each part separately using the following questions.

Analysis of (part/stage): _____

QUESTIONS TO ASK:

1. (**W2**) What worked well?

2. How do we know that?

3. (**W2**) What did not work as well as we hoped?

APPENDIX 8½C: *Tracking Success* WORKSHEET p.2 of 2

4. How do we know that?

5. What could we do differently next time to get closer to what God had in mind?

6. Who will be responsible to make this happen? ...or to remind us?

   Name: _____

   Phone: _____

   Email: _____

8½ Secrets: **BONUS SECRET #9**

SECRET #9 – BONUS

If you manage paid staff,

PLEASE NOTE

ALL of the strategies and suggestions in the <u>following</u> chapters apply to your paid staff as well as your Volunteers!

SECRET 1   Maximize the Power of Your (Staff) Resource
SECRET 2   Encourage with Credibility When Things Go Right
SECRET 3   Give Compassionate Criticism When Things Go Wrong
SECRET 4   Make Your Expectations Clear to Get the Results You Want
SECRET 5   Run Meetings that Don't Drive Your (Staff) Crazy
SECRET 6   Tap into Built-In Enthusiasm

_____

SECRET 8   Lead with Humility—Listen More, Talk Less
SECRET 8½ Strategically PLAN to Succeed!!

About the Author

JUNE KENNY—Since 1998, June Kenny has worked with pastors, churches and Christian non-profits to improve leadership skills, strengthen teamwork and increase volunteer impact. She also served as Director of Volunteer and Staff Development at a fast-paced church of 14,000 with over 130 staff and 2,000 volunteers.

With a Master's degree in Counseling, extensive training experience and a lifetime in Christian service (volunteer and otherwise), June has observed *best practices* firsthand and plenty of *not-so-best practices* that could and should be avoided.

Speaking Credentials:

- Delivered over 2,000 presentations to profit-based, non-profit and faith-based organizations
- Over 25 years as a corporate leadership trainer and program developer for General Motors, Ford, Chrysler, hospitals, state and federal agencies and manufacturing and service industry clients
- Regional and national conference speaker
- Clients included: Protestant denominational, Protestant non-denominational and Catholic churches (from 50 to 14,000 members). Christian non-profits included: LifeCare Christian Center (Recovery Ministry), Samaritan Counseling Center, Stonecroft Conference Center, Salvation Army ARC Executive Team, and others

Areas of Expertise:

Presentation and Meeting Facilitation Skills ≈ Interpersonal Communication ≈ Coaching Skills ≈ Team Development ≈ Managing Change ≈ Fundamentals of Leadership ≈ Conflict Management ≈ Effective Meetings ≈ Managing Stress ≈ Effective Delegation ≈ Time and Priority Management ≈ Executive Performance Coaching

June and her husband, Tim, are proud residents of Livonia, a great midwestern city, and active members of Faith Covenant Church, Farmington Hills, Michigan.

Much Appreciation:
to Family:
- My husband, Tim, for his unwavering encouragement. He persuaded me that I was the right person to get this valuable information from my office shelves into the hands of Ministry Leaders where it could make a difference.
- My daughter, Katie, extraordinary writer, sounding board, support, encourager, and cover designer who created the perfect "2-Second Story".
- My son-in-law, Jeff, for providing a role-model for exemplary ministry leadership. Pastors wished they had more like him!
- My son, Chris – attorney, negotiator, advisor on the nitty-gritty details of contracts and copyright, always supportive and always in my corner.
- My daughter-in-law, Ann – Scientific researcher extraordinaire who knows her way around data and Excel files which proved invaluable to me.
- My Mother-in-law, Irene Kenny, like a second mom, always supportive and proud of whatever I do.
- My parents, the late Frank and Ellen Weissenborn, who taught me that I could do anything I put my mind to. As avid readers, they would have been proud to know there was an author in the family.

to Professionals:
- My friend and former business partner, Joe Tabers at Productive Training Services *(www.productivetraining.com)* for allowing me to adapt our leadership materials to help Ministry Leaders make a greater impact through their Volunteers.
- Katie Phillips, Diana Pintar and Kelly Hawkins for superb professional editing.
- Linda Glaz, Christian Literary Agent, for believing this book needed to be written from the very beginning. You were such an encouragement along the way; it was unthinkable to give up.

and a huge *Thank You* to hundreds of friends and Volunteers over the last 7 1/2 years who provided never-ending encouragement, shared your stories and contributed invaluable advice. You helped me understand what leaders could do to grow from GOOD to GREAT. Together, through this book, we can make a difference. Thank you!

Made in the USA
Charleston, SC
29 December 2016